Jessica St. Arnault

THE
HOLY SPIRIT
TODAY

THE
HOLY SPIRIT
TODAY

BY
DICK IVERSON

Available from:

BIBLE TEMPLE PUBLISHING
9200 NE FREMONT
PORTLAND, OREGON 97220
(503) 253-9020 • (800) 777-6057

ISBN 0-914936-86-7
Printed in U.S.A.

Contents

Acknowledgement

I wish to acknowledge my deepest thanks and appreciation to Wayne Hayworth, a former instructor at Portland Bible College and a personal friend, for the countless hours he spent rewriting this present text from the original.

Introduction

There are few subjects harder to present from a highly doctrinal standpoint than the subject of the Holy Spirit. We realize that there are many worthwhile books which deal with the broad spectrum of the doctrine of the Holy Spirit and we are not attempting to improve on them. While, in the first part of this book, we have given a brief survey or skeleton of most of the vital teachings concerning the Holy Spirit, this is not our primary purpose. It is our goal to work within the framework of sound doctrine, yet to emphasize also instruction in the ways of the Spirit as He deals with man and manifests Himself to and through man. We will not deal only with the objective facts, but with the experiential and practical aspects as well.

We do not present these truths in any spirit of antagonism, this would be contrary to the Spirit of which we are speaking. We do present them with the earnest prayer that they may be a source of instruction and guidance to many hungry hearts. We have attempted to approach these truths from the standpoint of a *"present truth"* emphasis, which stresses that which is current and vital to the present move of God in the earth.

1

The Deity and Attributes of the Holy Spirit

Omniscience is ascribed to the Holy Spirit:

I Corinthians 2:10-11 -- *"But God hath revealed them unto us by His Spirit: for the Spirit searcheth all things, yea, the deep things of God. For what man knoweth the things of a man, save the spirit of man which is in him? even so the things of God knoweth no man, but the Spirit of God."*

This Scripture distinctly says that the Spirit searches all and knows all, even to the deep things of God.

John 14:26 -- *"But the Comforter, which is the Holy Ghost, whom the Father will send in My name, He shall teach you all things, and bring all things to your remembrance, whatsoever I have said unto you."*

If the Spirit teaches all, He must know all.

John 16:12-13 -- *"I have yet many things to say unto you, but ye cannot bear them now. Howbeit when He, the Spirit of truth, is come, He will guide you into all truth: for He shall not speak of Himself; but whatsoever He shall hear, that shall He speak: and He will show you things to come."*

Omnipresence is ascribed to the Holy Spirit:

Psalm 139:7-11 -- *"Whither shall I go from thy Spirit? or whither shall I flee from Thy presence? If I ascend up into heaven, Thou art there: if I make my bed in hell, behold, Thou art there. If I take the wings of the morning, and dwell* *in the uttermost parts of the sea; even there shall Thy hand lead me, and Thy right hand shall hold me. If I say, Surely the darkness shall cover me; even the night shall be light about me.*" (Couple this with Isaiah 66:1; Jeremiah 23:24.)

Omnipotence is ascribed to the Holy Spirit:

Luke 1:35 -- "*And the angel answered and said unto her, The Holy Ghost shall come upon thee, and the power of the Highest shall overshadow thee: therefore also that holy thing which shall be born of thee shall be called the Son of God.*"

We see in this verse the Holy Spirit and the power of God connected. (Also read I Thessalonians 1:5; I Corinthians 2:4.)

Eternity is ascribed to the Holy Spirit:

Hebrews 9:14 -- "*How much more shall the blood of Christ, who through the eternal Spirit offered Himself without spot to God, purge your conscience from dead works to serve the living God?*"

There are passages in the Old Testament that refer to God which are used in reference to the Holy Spirit in the New Testament.

* **Old Testament:** (Isaiah 6:8-10) -- "*Also I heard the voice of the Lord, saying, Whom shall I send, and who will go for us? Then said I, Here am I; send me. And He said, Go, and tell this people, Hear ye indeed, but understand not; and see ye indeed, but perceive not. Make the heart of this people fat, and make their ears heavy, and shut their eyes; lest they see with their eyes, and hear with their ears, and understand with their heart, and convert, and be healed.*"

2

* **New Testament:** (Acts 28:25-27) -- *"And when they agreed not among themselves, they departed, after that Paul had spoken one word, Well spake the Holy Ghost by Esaias the prophet unto our fathers, saying, Go unto this people, and say, Hearing ye shall hear, and shall not understand; and seeing ye shall see, and not perceive: For the heart of this people is waxed gross, and their ears are dull of hearing, and their eyes have they closed; lest they should see with their eyes, and hear with their ears, and understand with their heart, and should be converted, and I should heal them."*

Isaiah says it was the voice of the *"Lord,"* yet Paul says it was the Holy Spirit. (Compare with Hebrews 3:7-8.)

The name of the Holy Spirit is coupled with those of the Father and the Son:

I Corinthians 12:4-6 -- *"Now there are diversities of gifts, but the same Spirit. And there are differences of administrations, but the same Lord. And there are diversities of operations, but it is the same God which worketh all in all."*

Matthew 28:19 -- *"Go ye therefore, and teach all nations, baptizing them in the name of the Father, and of the Son, and of the Holy Ghost."*

II Corinthians 13:14 -- *"The grace of the Lord Jesus Christ, and the love of God, and the communion of the Holy Ghost, be with you all. Amen."*

The Holy Spirit is in fact spoken of as synonymous with God:

Acts 5:3-4 -- *"But Peter said, Ananias, why hath Satan filled thine heart to lie to the Holy Ghost, and to keep back part of the price of the land? While it remained, was it not thine*

3

own? and after it was sold, was it not in thine own power? why hast thou conceived this thing in thine heart? thou hast not lied unto men, but unto God."

2

The Personality of the Holy Spirit

The Holy Spirit has personality, though not a body of flesh. Personality is that which possesses intelligence, feeling, and will. When one possesses the characteristics, properties and qualities of personality, then personality can be attributed to that being. Personality, when used in reference to divine beings, cannot be measured by human standards.

Why is the doctrine of the personality of the Holy Spirit important?

* It is important from the standpoint of worship and recognition:

   If we think of Him as an abstract or impersonal influence or power, we are robbing a Divine Person of the worship, love and recognition which are His due:

* It is important from the practical standpoint:

   If He is thought of as merely influence or power, we will say, *"How can I get ahold of it and use it?"* But if we recognize Him as a Divine Person, our thoughts will be, *"How can the Holy Spirit get ahold of me and use me?"* This brings humility instead of self-exaltation.

* It is important from the standpoint of experience:

   You know that you actually have a person of the Godhead indwelling you, not just a power or influence. This leads to that *"communion with the Holy Ghost"* Paul referred to in II Corinthians 13:14.

Why is the doctrine of the personality of the Holy Spirit questioned?

* Because, contrasted with the other persons of the Godhead, the Spirit seems impersonal:

  His acts and works are more mystical and secret. He only appears as theophanies (divine manifestations) instead of in His own native body. So much is said of His influence, graces, power, gifts, that we are prone to think of Him as an influence or some kind of agent rather than as a person. These, however, are merely descriptions of His operations.

* Because of the names given to the Holy Spirit:

  He is called breath, wind, power, oil, etc. In view of this, many are led to believe that the Holy Spirit is an impersonal influence emanating from God the Father.

* Because He is not usually associated with the Father and Son in the greetings and salutations of the New Testament books. However, if He were associated with them in even one case, it would either be blasphemy or the revelation of a truth (see Matthew 28:19).

* Because the word *"spirit"* is neuter:

  It comes from the same Greek word used for *"wind."* Notice that because of this, some translations use the neuter pronoun *"itself"* instead of *"Himself"* in some passages (Romans 8:16, 26).

What is proof of the personality of the Holy Spirit?

* Distinctive marks or characteristics of personality are ascribed to the Holy Spirit:

  Knowledge -- (I Corinthians 2:11) -- *"For what man*

knoweth the things of a man, save the spirit of man which is in him? even so the things of God knoweth no man, but the Spirit of God."

He reveals what He himself knows: He is not just a reflector.

Will -- (I Corinthians 12:11) -- *"But all these worketh that one and the selfsame Spirit, dividing to every man severally as He will."*

One great secret of having the Spirit manifest Himself to and through us is to cooperate with His will.

Romans 8:27 -- *"And He that searcheth the hearts knoweth what is the mind of the Spirit, because He maketh intercession for the saints according to the will of God."*

Romans 8:27 shows us the Spirit knows the will of God and prays through us according to God's will.

Mind -- (Romans 8:27) -- *"And He that searcheth the hearts knoweth what is the mind of the Spirit, because He maketh intercession for the saints according to the will of God."*

The Greek word for *"mind"* has the connotation of "thought and purpose."

Love -- (Romans 15:30) -- *"Now I beseech you, brethren, for the Lord Jesus Christ's sake, and for the love of the Spirit, that ye strive together with me in your prayers to God for me."*

Romans 5:5 shows us that the Spirit is the one who pours love into the hearts of Christians. The Spirit is motivated by love in His ministry of leading men to Christ. Without the Spirit, the cross stands inert. He makes it real in personal experience.

Intelligence and Goodness -- (Nehemiah 9:20) -- *"Thou gavest also Thy good Spirit to instruct them, and withheldest* *not Thy manna from their mouth, and gavest them water for their thirst."*

Grief -- (Ephesians 4:30) -- *"And grieve not the Holy Spirit of God, whereby ye are sealed unto the day of redemption."*

The Holy Spirit is a person who is intensely sensitive to sin. He sees our very thoughts and is grieved beyond expression at our sin. This is a great incentive to walk a holy life.

* Actions are ascribed to the Holy Spirit which only a person can perform:

He Searches -- (I Corinthians 2:10) -- *"But God hath revealed them unto us by His Spirit: for the Spirit searcheth all things, yea, the deep things of God."*

He Prays -- (Romans 8:26) -- *"Likewise the Spirit also helpeth our infirmities: for we know not what we should pray as we ought: but the Spirit itself maketh intercession for us with groanings which cannot be uttered."*

Think of our tremendous security: Jesus Christ our advocate in heaven, and the Holy Spirit here on earth.

He Teaches -- (John 14:26) -- *"But the Comforter, which is the Holy Ghost, whom the Father will send in My name, He shall teach you all things, and bring all things to your remembrance, whatsoever I have said unto you."*

He Speaks -- (John 16:13) -- *"Howbeit when He, the Spirit of truth, is come, He will guide you unto all truth: for He shall not speak of Himself; but whatsoever He shall hear, that shall He speak: and He will show you things to come."*

He Gives Testimony -- (John 15:26) -- *"But when the Comforter is come, whom I will send unto you from the Father, even the Spirit of truth, which proceedeth from the Father, He shall testify of me."*

He Guides -- (John 16:13) -- *"Howbeit when He, the Spirit of truth, is come, He will guide you unto all truth: for He shall not speak of Himself; but whatsoever He shall hear, that shall He speak: and He will show you things* to come."

* An office was predicted for the Holy Spirit which could only be predicted for a person:

Comforter -- (John 14:16-17) -- *"And I will pray the Father, and He shall give you another Comforter, that He may abide with you forever; even the Spirit of truth; whom the world cannot receive, because it seeth Him not, neither knoweth Him: but ye know Him; for He dwelleth with you, and shall be in you."*

The word *"comforter"* comes from the Greek *"parakletos"* and literally means *"one called to one's side or aid."* It suggests the capability and adaptability of giving aid. It was used in court in reference to a legal assistant, counsel for the defense, or advocate. It speaks strongly of one who pleads another's cause.

The Spirit came as *"another"* comforter, or one who would take the place of Christ as He was when He walked among His disciples. This required a person, and not just an abstract impersonal influence.

* Personal pronouns are used in reference to the Holy Spirit:

John 16:7-8 -- *"Nevertheless I tell you the truth; It is expedient for you that I go away: for if I go not away, the Comforter will not come unto you; but if I depart, I will send Him unto you. And when He is come, He will reprove the world of sin, and of righteousness, and of judgment."*

John 16:7-15 -- The masculine pronoun *"He"* is used twelve times.

The Greek word for *"spirit"* (pneuma), is neuter, yet Jesus, referring to the Holy Spirit, used masculine pronouns.

* The Scriptures show that there is a distinction between the Father and the Son and the Spirit:

John 14:26 -- *"But the Comforter, which is the Holy Ghost, whom the Father will send in My name, He shall teach you all things, and bring all things to your remembrance, whatsoever I have said unto you."*

Luke 3:21-22 -- *"Now when all the people were baptized, it came to pass, that Jesus also being baptized, and praying, the heaven was opened, and the Holy Ghost descended in a bodily shape like a dove upon Him, and a voice from heaven, which said, Thou art my beloved Son; in Thee I am well pleased."*

John 15:26 -- *"But when the Comforter is come, whom I will send unto you from the Father, even the Spirit of truth, which proceedeth from the Father, He shall testify of Me."* (See also John 14:13-14; 8:29; 6:29.)

Again and again, the Bible draws the clearest possible distinction between the Holy Spirit and the Father and the Son. They are, by an incomprehensible mystery, separate personalities, having mutual relation to one another, acting upon one another, speaking of and to one another, applying the pronouns of the second and third persons to one another.

Our attempts to simplify this mystery and explain it philosophically is in reality an attempt to put the infinite realm of God into the form of finite thought. It is best to recognize the statements of the Word and leave it at that. The Trinity is large, incomprehensible and unexplainable to man's present mentality. Most arguments on this subject become so highly academic and hypothetical that they lose all bearing to practicality, and become pointless to the Christian life, as well as endless to those involved.

3

The Title and Symbols of the Holy Spirit

Names:

The Father and the Son have certain names ascribed to them setting forth their nature and work. Likewise, the Holy Spirit has names which indicate His character and work.

While the following is probably not a comprehensive list, it does give all the major names in Scripture.

* **The Spirit of God** -- (Genesis 1:2) -- *"And the earth was without form, and void; and darkness was upon the face of the deep. And the Spirit of God moved upon the face of the waters."*

* **The Holy Spirit** -- (Luke 11:13) -- *"If ye then, being evil, know how to give good gifts unto your children: how much more shall your heavenly Father give the Holy Spirit to them that ask Him?"*

* **The Spirit of Grace** -- (Hebrews 10:29) -- *"Of how much sorer punishment, suppose ye, shall be thought worthy, who hath trodden under foot the Son of God, and hath counted the blood of the covenant, wherewith he was sanctified, an unholy thing, and hath done despite unto the Spirit of grace?"*

* **The Spirit of Burning** -- (Isaiah 4:4) -- *"When the Lord shall have washed away the filth of the daughters of Zion, and shall have purged the blood of Jerusalem from the midst thereof by the spirit of judgment, and by the spirit of burning."*

Here we see the searching, illuminating, refining, dross-consuming character of the Spirit. He burns up the dross in our lives as He takes complete possession of us. (See also Matthew 3:11-12.)

* **The Spirit of Truth** -- (John 14:17) -- *"Even the Spirit of truth; whom the world cannot receive, because it seeth Him not, neither knoweth Him: but ye know Him; for He dwelleth with you, and shall be in you."*

John 16:13 -- *"Howbeit when He, the Spirit of truth, is come, He will guide you into all truth; for He shall not speak of Himself; but whatsoever He shall hear, that shall He speak: and He will show you things to come."*

He possesses the truth, reveals the truth, leads into the truth, testifies to and defends the truth, thus opposing the spirit of error.

* **The Spirit of Life** -- (Romans 8:2) -- *"For the law of the Spirit of life in Christ Jesus hath made me free from the law of sin and death."*

The Spirit introduces us to the realm of eternal life, and He is the dynamic in the believer's experience that leads him into life, liberty, and power.

* **The Spirit of Wisdom and Revelation** -- (Ephesians 1:17) -- *"That the God of our Lord Jesus Christ, the Father of glory, may give unto you the spirit of wisdom and revelation in the knowledge of Him."*

Wisdom and knowledge and revelation are the results of being filled with the Spirit. (See also Isaiah 11:2; 61:1-2.)

* **The Spirit of Promise** -- (Ephesians 1:13) -- *"In whom ye also trusted, after that ye heard the word of truth, the gospel of your salvation: in whom also after that ye believed, ye were sealed with that Holy Spirit of promise."*

Joel 2:28 -- *"And it shall come to pass afterward, that I will pour out My Spirit upon all flesh; and your sons and your daughters shall prophesy, your old men shall dream dreams, your young men shall see visions."*

Ezekiel 36:27 -- *"And I will put My Spirit within you, and cause you to walk in My statutes, and ye shall keep My judgments, and do them."*

The receiving of the Spirit is the fulfillment of Christ's promise to send another comforter. (See Luke 24:49; Acts 1:4; Galatians 3:14.)

* **The Spirit of Glory** -- (I Peter 4:14) -- *"If ye be reproached for the name of Christ, happy are ye; for the Spirit of glory and of God resteth upon you: on their part He is evil spoken of, but on your part He is glorified."*

* **The Spirit of Christ** -- (I Corinthians 3:16) -- *"Know ye not that ye are the temple of God, and that the Spirit of God dwelleth in you?"*

Romans 8:9 -- *"But ye are not in the flesh, but in the Spirit, if so be that the Spirit of God dwell in you. Now if any man have not the Spirit of Christ, he is none of His."*

* **The Comforter** -- (John 14:16) -- *"And I will pray the Father, and He shall give you another Comforter, that He may abide with you for ever."*

"Comforter" means one called to stand by another; to always be between us and the enemy, giving aid and help.

* **The Spirit of Adoption** -- (Romans 8:15) -- *"For ye have not received the spirit of bondage again to fear; but ye have received the Spirit of adoption, whereby we cry, Abba, Father."*

Symbols:

Remember, these are not names, rather symbols. These symbols bring out various aspects of the operations and nature of the Holy Spirit.

* **Fire** -- (Isaiah 4:4) -- *"When the Lord shall have washed away the filth of the daughters of Zion, and shall have purged the blood of Jerusalem from the midst thereof by the spirit of judgment, and by the spirit of burning."*

Matthew 3:11 -- *"I indeed baptize you with water unto repentance: but He that cometh after Me is mightier than I, whose shoes I am not worthy to bear: He shall baptize you with the Holy Ghost, and with fire."*

The main emphasis of fire in the Scripture is purging, purification, burning out dross, etc. Fire will be involved in final judgment.

* **Wind** -- (Ezekiel 37:7-10) -- *"So I prophesied as I was commanded: as I prophesied, there was a noise, and behold a shaking, and the bones came together, bone to his bone. And when I beheld, lo, the sinews, and the flesh came up upon them, and the skin covered them above: but there was no breath in them. Then said He unto me, Prophesy unto the wind, prophesy, son of man, and say to the wind, Thus saith the Lord God; Come from the four winds, O breath, and breathe upon these slain, that they may live. So I prophesied as he commanded me and the breath came unto them, and they lived, and stood up upon their feet, an exceeding great army."*

John 3:8 -- *"The wind bloweth where it listeth, and thou hearest the sound thereof, but canst not tell whence it cometh, and whither it goeth: so is every one that is born of the Spirit."*

Acts 2:2-3 -- *"And suddenly there came a sound from heaven as of a rushing mighty wind, and it filled all the house where they were sitting. And there appeared unto* *them cloven tongues like as of fire, and it sat upon each of them."*

Wind symbolizes the regenerative work of the Spirit and is indicative of His mysterious, independent, penetrating operation.

* **Water** -- (John 7:38-39) -- *"He that believed on Me, as the Scripture hath said, out of his belly shall flow rivers of living water. (But this spake He of the Spirit, which they that believe on Him should receive: for the Holy Ghost was not yet given; because that Jesus was not yet glorified.)"*

John 4:14 -- *"But whosoever drinketh of the water that I shall give him shall never thirst; but the water that I shall give him shall be in him a well of water springing up into everlasting life."*

(See also Exodus 17:6 with I Corinthians 10:1-3, Ezekiel 36:25-27 with Titus 3:5.)

Water cleanses and washes away defilement; it purifies; it satisfies the thirst; it refreshes and maintains life and makes fruitful. Without water, there would be no natural life; without the Spirit there would be no spiritual life.

The Spirit is as *"living water"* or *"life-producing"* water, it must be continually bubbling up or flowing--not a stagnant marsh or reservoir in our lives.

* **A Seal** -- (Ephesians 1:13) -- *"In whom ye also trusted, after that ye heard the word of truth, the gospel of your salvation: in whom also after that ye believed, ye were sealed with that Holy Spirit of promise."*

The seal speaks of a pledge or an earnest. God will claim us as His and complete the purchase of His possession (Ephesians 1:14).

The message of the seal gives us great assurance and establishes the fact beyond any doubt or wavering that we are His.

* **Oil** -- In the Old Testament, all the prophetic, kingly, and priestly ministers were anointed with special oil. This anointing represented a separation and sanctification of the person unto a holy purpose. It also represented the divine enablement and qualification for that ministry. No one dared enter one of these particular ministries without it.

Acts 10:38 -- *"How God anointed Jesus of Nazareth with the Holy Ghost and with power: who went about doing good, and healing all that were oppressed of the devil; for God was with Him."*

This Scripture connects the qualifying, enabling, empowering, anointing with the ministry of the Holy Spirit in the life of Christ.

I John 2:27 -- *"But the anointing which ye have received of Him abideth in you, and ye need not that any man teach you: but as the same anointing teacheth you of all things, and is truth, and is no lie, and even as it hath taught you, ye shall abide in Him."*

This reference shows it as also an experience for the life of the believer. By looking at John 14:26 and I Corinthians 2:13, we can identify the anointing with the Holy Spirit because He is said to be the one who teaches us. (See also Psalm 89:20; 92:10; Matthew 25:3.)

Oil also speaks to us of strengthening, healing, soothing, and illumination.

* **The Dove** -- (Matthew 3:16) -- *"And Jesus, when He was baptized, when up straightway out of the water: and, lo, the heavens were opened unto Him, and He saw the Spirit of God descending like a dove, and lighting upon Him."*

The dove nature of the Holy Spirit is a beautiful truth. It speaks to us of gentleness, tenderness, sensitivity, innocence, purity, peace, and patience.

4

The Holy Spirit in Relation to Creation, Nature, and Humanity as a Whole

As we study the interrelatedness of the members of the Trinity, we discover that the Holy Spirit and the spoken Word of God work hand in hand. Everything God does is spoken into existence by the creative word. Christ is the Word personified (Revelation 19:13; John 1:14).

Incidentally, this shows us the importance of our speech and confession and the necessity of prayer. We must speak the creative word before the Spirit is released to work miracles.

In the beginning, the Spirit brooded over the face of the waters, yet the earth remained a chaotic mess until God SPOKE. Then the Word and the Spirit combined to bring cosmos out of chaos. We could say, then, that the Spirit is the executive agent of the Godhead; the One having to do with the carrying out, executing, or putting into effect the affairs of God. This means He possesses the power and resources necessary to put God's Word into effect.

Let us keep these thoughts in mind as we proceed in this study. That all of the Trinity was involved in all of the creation is undeniable. We might take to heart the statement in Genesis 1:26 where God said, *"Let Us make man in Our image and after Our likeness."* This shows the plural involvement of the Godhead.

Creation and nature:

* **The Universe** -- (Psalm 33:6) -- *"By the word of the Lord were the heavens made; and all the host of them by the breath of His mouth."*

By comparing Genesis 1:1 with the rest of the chapter, which demonstrates how the Lord creates, we can conclude that the Spirit was involved in the same way in the creation of the entire universe.

* **The Earth** -- (Genesis 1:2) -- *"And the earth was without form, and void; and darkness was upon the face of the deep. And the Spirit of God moved upon the face of the waters."*

Psalm 104:30 -- *"Thou sendest forth Thy Spirit, they are created: and Thou renewest the face of the earth."*

* **Man** -- (Job 33:4) -- *"The Spirit of God hath made me, and the breath of the Almighty hath given me life."*

Genesis 1:26 -- *"And God said, Let Us make man in Our image, after Our likeness: and let them have dominion over the fish of the sea, and over the fowl of the air, and over the cattle, and over the earth, and over every creeping thing that creepeth upon the earth."*

* **Sea Life** -- (Psalm 104:24-30) -- *"O Lord, how manifold are Thy works! in wisdom Thou hast made them all: the earth is full of Thy riches. So is this great and wide sea, wherein are things creeping innumerable, both small and great beasts. There go the ships: there is that leviathan, whom Thou hast made to play therein. These wait all upon Thee; that Thou mayest give them their meat in due season. That thou givest them they gather: Thou openest Thine hand, they are filled with good. Thou hidest Thy face, they are troubled: Thou takest away their breath, they die, and return to their dust. Thou sendest forth Thy spirit, they are created: and Thou renewest the face of the earth."*

If this is true of sea life, it would be only normal to

assume that it relates to all other forms of life as well.

* **Preservation of Nature** -- (Hebrews 1:3) -- *"Who being the brightness of His glory, and the express image of His person, and upholding all things by the word of His power, when He had by Himself purged our sins, sat down on the right hand of the Majesty on high."*

Again, we can deduce from knowledge of the operations of the Holy Trinity throughout the Word, that the word of His power, here referred to as *"up-holding"* (bearing up or carrying) all things, is being activated and executed by the Holy Spirit. The *"all things"* refers back to verse 2 which speaks of the making of the worlds. So God, in the beginning, not only spoke the worlds into beginnings, but the same words carried the sense of continuity, establishing what we call *"laws of nature."*

(See Genesis 1 on each creative pronouncement of the seven days -- all these are still in effect.)

Humanity as a whole:

Now that man and the universe have been created and set into motion, and man finds himself alienated from God, what is the relationship of the Holy Spirit to humanity?

John 16:7-11 seems to summarize it quite thoroughly: *"Nevertheless I tell you the truth; It is expedient for you that I go away: for if I go not away, the Comforter will not come unto you; but if I depart, I will send Him unto you. And when He is come, He will reprove the world of sin, and of righteousness, and of judgment: of sin, because they believe not on Me; of righteousness, because I go to My Father, and ye see Me no more; of judgment, because the prince of this world is judged."*

* **"Reprove the world of sin..."**

Verse 9 shows that the root of sin is not believing in

Christ, which constitutes a rejection of the Gospel.

◢ The Spirit reproves or "_convicts_" men of sin through the Word and by arousing their hearts and consciences.

"_Reprove_," as used here, is a legal term and carried the idea of a judge summing up the evidence and convicting one as guilty. And by so doing, He puts to silence all justification for the guilty party. One then stands exposed and proven guilty, the verdict being clearly pronounced by the Spirit to his own heart.

* **"Of righteousness, because I go to My Father and ye see Me no more..."**

This may be understood from two standpoints:

Christ's personal righteousness --

The evidence of this was the fact that He had risen from the dead and had gone to the Father. The fact that God raised Him and placed Him at His own right hand was divine evidence and proof that He was the "_righteous Servant_" of God, and not a criminal or impostor, as He was accused of being. His resurrection, therefore, became the seal of authentication.

This was illustrated in Acts 2:32-37 in Peter's Pentecostal message. In it he showed that, though Christ was crucified as a criminal, He was proven righteous. It was then that the people's hearts were pricked and they asked, "_What shall we do?_"

Christ's righteousness made available to man --

— The Spirit must convince men of the availability of divine righteousness and their own need of it.

His resurrection and acceptance by God also assures us of justification through Christ. If He had not gone to the Father, then we could not believe His message.

* "And of judgment, because the prince of this world is judged..."

—The Spirit witnesses to and convinces men that Satan's power is broken.

The same thought is brought out in John 12:31, "*now shall the prince of this world be cast out.*"

The death of Christ judicially overthrew Satan as far as His dominion over the souls of men is concerned. He is no longer able to deceive the nations or enslave them in spiritual darkness (Hebrews 2:14-15; I John 3:8; Colossians 2:15).

The fact that Christ has broken the power of Satan is also a sure token of the judgment that awaits all who do not accept Him. If the power of Satan himself was subdued by Christ, then all can be certain that no other power can stand before Him. Judgment is inevitable and will certainly come. There will be no escaping the judgment.

It is the ministry of the Spirit to bear witness to men of their **sin** and of Christ's **righteousness**, and that "*it is appointed unto men once to die, but after that the judgment.*"

After preaching all these truths before the Sanhedrin, Peter states, "*And we are His witnesses of these things; and so is also the Holy Ghost*" (Acts 5:32).

We should mention, too, that this was also the general ministry of the Spirit in the Old Testament. Genesis 6:3 tells us, "*My Spirit shall not always strive with man.*"

5

The Holy Spirit in Relation to the Believer

Regenerates:

Titus 3:5 -- *"Not by works of righteousness which we have done, but according to His mercy He saved us, by the washing of regeneration, and renewing of the Holy Ghost."*

The Greek word for regeneration here is *palingenesia,* and means "to be birthed again." It speaks of the communication of new life. (See II Corinthians 3:6.)

John 3:3 -- *"Jesus answered and said unto him, Verily, verily, I say unto thee, Except a man be born again, he cannot see the kingdom of God."*

I Corinthians 12:13 -- *"For by one Spirit we are all baptized into one body, whether we be Jews or Gentiles, whether we be bond or free; and have been all made to drink into one Spirit."*

NOTE: By comparing these references with I Peter 1:23 we again see that the two operating powers are the Word and the Spirit. This truth applies to the new birth, the creation, and all of the works of God.

It is therefore vitally important that we be equipped with the Word so that the Spirit will be quickened and released to work. The Spirit is not released to save men by the preaching of any gospel, but rather *THE* Gospel. The same is true concerning all the truths of the Bible. If we want to see the Spirit released to perform His work, we must be speaking the right Word.

Indwells the believer:

John 14:17 -- *"Even the Spirit of truth; whom the world cannot receive, because it seeth Him not, neither knoweth Him: but ye know Him; for He dwelleth with you, and shall be in you."*

Romans 8:9 -- *"But ye are not in the flesh, but in the Spirit, if so be that the Spirit of God dwell in you. Now if any man have not the Spirit of Christ, he is none of His."*

II Timothy 1:14 -- *"That good thing which was committed unto thee keep by the Holy Ghost which dwelleth in us."*

To *"dwell"* speaks of taking up permanent residence. It is the same as *to live in* -- just as a family lives in a house.

Some have taken the position that the Holy Spirit's personal presence does not actually live in the believer, but that He is present in a mystical *"omnipresent"* sense. This, of course, is a denial of a very central teaching of the New Covenant and is to be rejected.

Liberates the believer from the power of sin and death:

* **The added dimension of the power of the Holy Spirit operating in our practical lives.**

  Romans 8:1-2 -- *"There is therefore now no condemnation to them which are in Christ Jesus, who walk not after the flesh, but after the Spirit. For the law of the Spirit of life in Christ Jesus hath made me free from the law of sin and death."*

  Ephesians 3:16 -- *"That He would grant you, according to the riches of His glory, to be strengthened with might by His Spirit in the inner man."*

24

Ephesians 1:19 -- *"And what is the exceeding greatness of His power to us-ward who believe, according to the working of His mighty power."*

This shows us that we are no longer limited to natural powers in order to live up to God's standards, but rather, God has planted within us all of the spiritual resources of the Holy Spirit. We can no longer say that we are *"just human,"* for we are humans possessed by the Holy Spirit.

Through this added dynamic of the Holy Spirit in our lives, God has broken our bondage to the enslavement of sin. We are now in another Kingdom and enabled to serve a new master (Romans 6:13-18).

* Through the renewing of our minds.

Romans 12:1-2 -- *"I beseech you therefore, brethren, by the mercies of God, that ye present your bodies a living sacrifice, holy, acceptable unto God, which is your reasonable service. And be not conformed to this world: but be ye transformed by the renewing of your mind, that ye may prove what is that good, and acceptable, and perfect will of God."*

I Corinthians 3:18 -- *"Let no man deceive himself. If any man among you seemeth to be wise in the world, let him become a fool, that he may be wise."*

(See also I Corinthians 4:16; Colossians 3:10; Ephesians 4:23.)

This involves transformation and change in the realms of the heart, attitudes and personality.

We are transformed and brought to maturity on a *relative* and *continuing* basis. By *relative,* we mean that a person saved for one week will not be required to have the same level of maturity as someone saved for five years. The demands of God on our lives follow the principle, "to whom much is given, much shall be required." By *continuing* we mean that the Scriptures point out that being brought to maturity is a process, not a crisis.

The expressed will and purpose of God is to bring each Christian to the image of His Son (Romans 8:29; Colossians 3:10). This takes place here in this life, and not suddenly at the second coming. God wants us to so yield to His changing in this life that all that will need to be changed at the second coming will be our bodies.

The emphasis of the Scriptures is not the idea of being changed in the eternities of the future, but rather during this life. The Spirit becomes life and liberation within us working out the very image of Christ (Galatians 4:19; 2:20).

Gives assurance of salvation:

Romans 8:16 -- *"The Spirit itself beareth witness with our spirit, that we are the children of God."*

Ephesians 1:13-14 -- *"In whom ye also trusted, after that ye heard the word of truth, the gospel of your salvation: in whom also after that ye believed, ye were sealed with that Holy Spirit of promise, which is the earnest of our inheritance until the redemption of the purchased possession, unto the praise of His glory."*

He constantly bears witness of our relationship with God. We actually go through many experiences with the Lord through the Spirit. It is a real active relationship and not just a doctrine.

Fills the believer:

Acts 2:4 -- *"And they were filled with the Holy Ghost, and began to speak with other tongues, as the Spirit gave them utterance."*

Acts 4:31 -- *"And when they had prayed, the place was shaken where they were assembled together; and they were all filled with the Holy Ghost, and they spake the word of God with boldness."*

Ephesians 5:18 -- *"And be not drunk with wine, wherein is excess; but be filled with the Spirit."*

Notice that in this verse being filled with the Spirit is not presented as an option, but an imperative.

At least nine times the New Testament speaks of being filled with the Spirit. It speaks of being inwardly pervaded. This means "to completely or copiously fill and imbue and influence."

Equips the believer for service:

Acts 1:8 -- *"But ye shall receive power, after that the Holy Ghost is come upon you: and ye shall be witnesses unto Me both in Jerusalem, and in all Judea, and in Samaria, and unto the uttermost part of the earth."*

I Corinthians 12:7-11 -- *"But the manifestation of the Spirit is given to every man to profit withal. For to one is given by the Spirit the word of wisdom; to another the word of knowledge by the same Spirit; to another faith by the same Spirit; to another the gifts of healing by the same Spirit; to another the working of miracles; to another prophecy; to another discerning of spirits; to another divers kinds of tongues; to another the interpretation of tongues: But all these worketh that one and the selfsame Spirit, dividing to every man severally as He will."*

I Corinthians 12:7-11 lists the various gifts of the Spirit distributed among the saints for ministry. We will be dealing later with each of these in detail. These could be called the munitions for God's enterprise. It is through these that the Spirit ministers to the Body, and manifests Himself.

(See also Romans 12:3-8; Matthew 25:15; Ephesians 4:11.)

Produces Christlike fruit in the believer:

Galatians 5:22-23 -- *"But the fruit of the Spirit is love, joy, peace, longsuffering, gentleness, goodness, faith, meekness, temperance: against such there is no law."*

Philippians 1:11 -- *"Being filled with the fruits of righteousness, which are by Jesus Christ, unto the glory and praise of God."*

James 3:17 -- *"But the wisdom that is from above is first pure, then peaceable, gentle, and easy to be intreated, full of mercy and good fruits, without partiality, and without hypocrisy."*

This speaks of the very nature and personality of the Lord being expressed through believers.

(See also Colossians 1:10; Psalm 92:13-14; Matthew 13:23; John 15:2; Romans 5:3-4; II Corinthians 6:6; I Peter 1:5-7.)

Makes possible all forms of communion with God:

* **Prayer** -- (Jude 20) -- *"But ye, beloved, building up yourselves on your most holy faith, praying in the Holy Ghost."*

  Romans 8:26 -- *"Likewise the Spirit also helpeth our infirmities: for we know not what we should pray for as we ought: but the Spirit itself maketh intercession for us with groanings which cannot be uttered."*

* **Worship** -- (Philippians 3:3) -- *"For we are the circumcision, which worship God in the Spirit, and rejoice in Christ Jesus, and have no confidence in the flesh."*

  John 4:23-24 -- *"But the hour cometh, and now is, when the* *true worshippers shall worship the Father in spirit and in truth: for the Father seeketh such to worship Him. God is a spirit: and they that worship Him must worship Him in spirit and in truth."*

* **Spiritual singing --** (Ephesians 5:18-20) -- *"And be not drunk with wine, wherein is excess; but be filled with the Spirit; speaking to yourselves in psalms and hymns and spiritual songs, singing and making melody in your heart to the Lord; giving thanks always for all things unto God and the Father in the name of our Lord Jesus Christ."*

* **Colossians 3:16 --** *"Let the word of Christ dwell in you richly in all wisdom; teaching and admonishing one another in psalms and hymns and spiritual songs, singing with grace in your hearts to the Lord."*

* **I Corinthians 14:15 --** *"What is it then? I will pray with the Spirit, and I will pray with the understanding also: I will sing with the Spirit, and I will sing with the understanding also."*

Guides the believer's life and ministry:

Romans 8:14 -- *"For as many as are led by the Spirit of God, they are the sons of God."*

John 16:13 -- *"Howbeit when He, the Spirit of truth, is come, He will guide you into all truth: for He shall not speak of Himself; but whatsoever He shall hear, that shall He speak: and He will show you things to come."*

This shows us that He guides us into truth.

Acts 10:19-20 -- *"While Peter thought on the vision, the Spirit said unto him, Behold, three men seek thee. Arise therefore, and get thee down, and go with them, doubting nothing: for I have sent them."*

This shows us that He controls the movement of believers in their ministry. (See also Acts 16:6.)

Acts 13:2 -- *"As they ministered to the Lord, and fasted, the Holy Ghost said, Separate Me Barnabas and Saul for the work whereunto I have called them."*

He directs in the selection and thrusting out of leaders.

Quickens the believer's body at the resurrection:

Romans 8:11 -- *"But if the Spirit of Him that raised up Jesus from the dead dwell in you, He that raised up Christ from the dead shall also quicken your mortal bodies by his Spirit that dwelleth in you."*

The word *"quicken"* here means *"to make alive."* It is the new life which our bodies will take on, rather than physical healing or preservation, that is being referred to here, similar to the reference to the bodily resurrection of Christ in the same verse. (See also I Peter 3:18.)

II Corinthians 3:18 -- *"But we all, with open face beholding as in a glass the glory of the Lord, are changed into the same image from glory to glory even as by the Spirit of the Lord."*

It will be the Spirit who will also perform the final change. In fact, John 14:16 leads us to believe that the Spirit will abide in us even in eternity. Is it possible that blood will no longer animate this body, rather it will be animated by the Spirit?

The Holy Spirit in Relation to the Scriptures

The Holy Spirit authored the Scriptures:

II Peter 1:21 -- *"For the prophecy came not in old time by the will of man: but holy men of God spake as they were moved by the Holy Ghost."*

Revelation 2:7, 17, 29 -- *"He that hath an ear, let him hear what the Spirit saith unto the churches; to him that overcometh will I give to eat of the tree of life, which is in the midst of the paradise of God...He that hath an ear, let him hear what the Spirit saith unto the churches; To him that overcometh will I give to eat of the hidden manna, and will give him a white stone, and in the stone a new name written, which no man knoweth saving he that receiveth it...He that hath an ear, let him hear what the Spirit saith unto the churches..."*

In the Scriptures, there are around 3800 places where statements occur such as *"The Spirit entered into me," "Jehovah spoke unto Moses," "The Lord said to Isaiah," "The Word of the Lord came to Jeremiah,"* etc.

(See also Acts 1:16; II Timothy 3:16.)

The Spirit inspires the presentation of the Scriptures:

II Samuel 23:1-2 -- *"Now these be the last words of David. David the son of Jesse said, and the man who was raised up on high, the anointed of the God of Jacob, and the sweet psalmist of Israel, said, The Spirit of the Lord spake by me,* *and His word was in my tongue."*

I Timothy 2:4 -- *"Who will have all men to be saved, and to come unto the knowledge of the truth."*

Acts 4:8,13 -- *"Then Peter, filled with the Holy Ghost, said unto them, Ye rulers of the people, and elders of Israel...Now when they saw the boldness of Peter and John, and perceived that they were unlearned and ignorant men, they marvelled; and they took knowledge of them, that they had been with Jesus."*

Acts 6:10 -- *"And they were not able to resist the wisdom and the Spirit by which He spake."*

This speaks primarily of the anointing that is upon the one who is preaching the Word. Any minister of the Gospel can testify of the Spiritual unction which often accompanies the presentation of the Word.

(See also Matthew 10:20; Luke 4:18; I Timothy 4:1.)

The Spirit produces response to the Word that is presented:

Acts 2:37 -- *"Now when they heard this, they were pricked in their heart, and said unto Peter and to the rest of the apostles, Men and brethren, what shall we do?"*

Acts 13:42-43,48 -- *"And when the Jews were gone out of the synagogue, the Gentiles besought that these words might be preached to them the next sabbath. Now when the congregation was broken up, many of the Jews and religious proselytes followed Paul and Barnabas: who, speaking to them, persuaded them to continue in the grace of God...And when the Gentiles heard this, they were glad, and glorified the word of the Lord: and as many as were ordained to eternal life believed."*

Acts 12:24 -- *"But the word of God grew and multiplied."*

Acts 10:44 -- *"While Peter yet spake these words, the Holy Ghost fell on them which heard the word."*

(Also note Acts 17:1-4; I Peter 1:22; Acts 18:4-8.)

The Spirit quickens the Scriptures to the believer's understanding:

He is actively involved in imparting spiritual insights and illuminating the Word to the hearts and minds of believers. He does this within each believer to the degree of his maturity, experience, and yieldedness to walk in the Spirit.

John 6:63 -- *"It is the Spirit that quickeneth; the flesh profiteth nothing: the words that I speak unto you, they are spirit, and they are life."*

I Corinthians 2:10-14 -- *"But God hath revealed them unto us by His Spirit: for the Spirit searcheth all things, yea, the deep things of God. For what man knoweth the things of a man, save the spirit of man which is in him? even so the things of God knoweth no man, but the Spirit of God. Now we have received, not the spirit of the world, but the Spirit which is of God; that we might know the things that are freely given to us of God. Which things also we speak, not in the words which man's wisdom teacheth, but which the Holy Ghost teacheth; comparing spiritual things with spiritual. But the natural man receiveth not the things of the Spirit of God: for they are foolishness unto him: neither can he know them, because they are spiritually discerned."*

II Corinthians 3:6 -- *"Who also hath made us able ministers of the new testament; not of the letter, but of the Spirit: for the letter killeth, but the Spirit giveth life."*

Nehemiah 9:20 -- *"Thou gavest also thy good Spirit to instruct them, and withheldest not Thy manna from their mouth, and* *gavest them water for their thirst."*

I John 2:27 -- *"But the anointing which ye have received of Him abideth in you, and ye need not that any man teach you: but as the same anointing teacheth you of all things, and is truth, and is no lie, and even as it hath taught you, ye shall abide in Him."*

The contextual meaning of I John 2:27 is that the anointing will teach us truth from error. In other words, no one who is a liar or has the spirit of antichrist will be able to deceive us (vs. 16-26).

7

The Promise and Fulfillment of the Outpouring of the Holy Spirit

In order to see the significance of the outpouring of the Spirit on every believer, we must understand what the relationship of the Spirit was to God's people in Old Testament times.

In the Old Testament, it is said that men were *filled* with the Spirit (Exodus 28:3; 31:3; 35:31; Deuteronomy 34:9). We notice, however, that these were isolated cases and for a particular ministry.

It is also said that men had the Spirit in them (Numbers 27:18; Isaiah 63:11). David prayed, *"Take not Thy Holy Spirit from me"* (Psalm 51:11).

It is said that the Spirit came upon, or clothed men (Judges 6:34; Numbers 11:17, 25, 26; 24:2; Judges 11:29).

We do not have any information, however, that would lead us to believe that the Spirit's ministry in these men was anywhere near as extensive as it is toward the believer today. (Refer to Chapter 5.)

The predominant truth of the Old Testament is that the Spirit came upon, and even within, isolated men. Through these, God led the nation, delivered them from captivity, or performed some unusual and extraordinary job. But rather than being a general experience for all believers, it was confined to the judges, kings, prophets, priests, etc.

The promise of the outpouring:

* The witness of the prophets

The prophets spoke of a new day when God would put His Spirit upon and within all His people. In other words, that which had been the exceptional experience of the isolated few was to become the average for His people, plus an even greater relationship.

Ezekiel 36:24-27 -- *"For I will take you from among the heathen, and gather you out of all countries, and will bring you into your land. Then I will sprinkle clean water upon you, and ye shall be clean: from all your filthiness, and from all your idols, will I cleanse you. A new heart also will I give you, and a new spirit will I put within you: and I will take away the stony heart out of your flesh, and I will give you a heart of flesh. And I will put My Spirit within you, and cause you to walk in My statutes, and ye shall keep My judgments, and do them."*

Joel 2:28-29 -- *"And it shall come to pass afterward, that I will pour out My Spirit upon all flesh; and your sons and your daughters shall prophesy, your old men shall dream dreams, your young men shall see visions: and also upon the servants and upon the handmaids in those days will I pour out My Spirit."*

Ezekiel 37:14 -- *"And shall put My Spirit in you, and ye shall live, and I shall place you in your own land: then shall ye know that I the Lord have spoken it, and performed it, saith the Lord."*

* The witness of John the Baptist

Matthew 3:11-12 -- *"I indeed baptize you with water unto repentance: but He that cometh after me is mightier than I, whose shoes I am not worthy to bear: He shall baptize you with the Holy Ghost, and with fire. Whose fan is in His hand, and He will thoroughly purge His floor, and gather His*

*wheat into the garner; but He will burn up the chaff with
unquenchable fire."*

(Also Mark 1:8; Luke 3:16-18; John 1:29-34.)

* **The witness of Christ**

John 14:16-17, 26 -- *"And I will pray the Father, and He
shall give you another Comforter, that He may abide with
you forever; even the Spirit of truth; whom the world cannot
receive, because it seeth Him not, neither knoweth Him: but
ye know Him; for He dwelleth with you, and shall be in
you...But the Comforter; which is the Holy Ghost, whom
the Father will send in My name, He shall teach you all
things, and bring all things to your remembrance, whatsoever
I have said unto you."*

Acts 1:4, 8 -- *"And, being assembled together with them,
commanded them that they should not depart from
Jerusalem, but wait for the promise of the Father, which,
saith He, ye have heard of Me...But ye shall receive power,
after that the Holy Ghost is come upon you: and ye shall
be witnesses unto Me both in Jerusalem, and in all Judea,
and in Samaria, and unto the uttermost part of the earth."*

Luke 24:49 -- *"And, behold, I send the promise of My
Father upon you: but tarry ye in the city of Jerusalem, until
ye be endued with power from on high."*

(Also John 15:26-27; 16:7-14; 7:37-39.)

The fulfillment of the outpouring:

* **Pentecost** -- There can be no question that what happened
on the day of Pentecost, as is recorded in Acts, chapter 2,
was the initial fulfillment of what Christ promised and the
prophets had predicted. Peter confirms this in Acts 2:16,
"This is that which was spoken by the prophet Joel..." This
becomes God's own interpretation of Joel 2. Peter also

referred to these events as including the *"promise of the Father,"* or as Jesus called it, *"the promise of the Spirit."* In verses 38 and 39, He also taught that it was for them, their children, *"and to all that are afar off, even as many as the Lord our God shall call."*
Other references showing that the promised outpouring continued on include Acts 8:17; 9:17-18; 10:44; 11:15-17; 19:6.

References which refer to it are: I Corinthians 12:13; I John 2:20, 27; Romans 8:15; I Corinthians 2:12; 3:16; II Corinthians 1:22; 5:5; Galatians 4:6; Ephesians 1:13; I Thessalonians 4:8.

NOTE: Secular and sacred historians record multitudes of experiences of the Pentecostal outpouring. This is true of the post-apostolic fathers, and throughout history, and especially history since the Reformation.

8

The Baptism of the Holy Spirit as Distinct from Repentance and Water Baptism

Whether the baptism in the Spirit takes place at conversion is really not the final question, since it often happens that a person may repent, be baptized in water, and receive the Spirit all in the same day (Acts 2:38-39; 19:2 -- *"when ye believed,"* literal rendering). This is what actually took place at both Pentecost and the household of Cornelius.

It would be more accurate, however, to say that receiving the Spirit is generally subsequent to repentance, water baptism and remission of sins (Acts 2:38-39). Ideally, it is what we might call a distinct aspect of the conversion experience; just as distinct as repentance or water baptism. The reason that this ideal does not occur more is due to a lack of teaching, leadership, or not practicing the Word as it is written. We are not taught by Bible example to send people through a long probationary period before baptizing them in water, nor should we expect them to tarry for long periods before receiving the Spirit. On the contrary, they are to be baptized and receive the Spirit immediately by faith and on the basis of Christ's righteousness.

But even having said this, another question must be dealt with: *"What really happens when the baptism in the Spirit takes place?"* Or, *"What evidence should be expected at the time of receiving?"*

First, then, we will look at Scriptural evidences which show us that the baptism of the Spirit is an experience distinct in itself. Second, in the next lesson, we will look at the evidence of that experience.

A distinct experience by New Testament example:

* **Christ** -- We see this taught in the life of our Lord Himself. Before entering public ministry, He was baptized in water and the Spirit, *"descending like a dove, and lighting upon Him"* (Matthew 16-17; Mark 1:10-11; John 1:32-34).

Luke 4:1 records that after this experience, Jesus was *"full of the Holy Ghost."* It was only after this that He was empowered to defeat every test Satan presented to Him in the wilderness, and later, returned in the *"power of the Spirit"* (Luke 4:1-14).

While it is true that He was already the sinless Son of God and was *"strong in Spirit, filled with wisdom: and the grace of God was upon Him"* (Luke 2:40), it was not until after He received the Spirit that the prophecy of Isaiah was fulfilled: *"The Spirit of the Lord is upon Me, because He hath anointed Me to preach the gospel to the poor; He hath sent Me to heal the broken-hearted, to preach deliverance to the captives, and recovering of sight to the blind, to set at liberty them that are bruised"* (Luke 4:18; compare Isaiah 61:1). It was not until the Spirit came *"upon Him"* that He began to perform miracles and preach with great authority.

NOTE: The necessity of speaking in tongues was not upon Christ because God gave Him His Spirit without measure (John 3:34). *"For in Him dwelleth all the fulness of the Godhead bodily"* (Colossians 2:9; also 1:19). Yet in each of His followers dwells a *"measure"* (Ephesians 4:16). Regardless of how great a man's ministry, he still does not contain the *"fulness"* of the Spirit in the same scope as did Christ. The day will come when tongues will cease because the greater measure will come: *"that which is perfect"* (I Corinthians 13:8-10). Tongues are for the present order, to which Christ had no need to be accommodated. His communication with the Father was on a higher level.

* The disciples -- There can be no doubt that the disciples' names were already written in heaven (Luke 10:20) and that their lives had been touched by the Holy Spirit (John 20:21-23). And they certainly evidenced a strong spiritual experience prior to the outpouring at Pentecost. Evidence of this can be seen by the facts that (1) they were in unity and one accord (Acts 1:14); (2) they were in prayer and supplication (Acts 1:14); (3) they received revelation from the Scriptures (Acts 1:15-22); (4) they were continually in the temple praising and blessing God (Luke 24:53); (5) they were absolutely obedient to the command of Christ to wait for the promise of the Father, even though it meant waiting in prayer and praise for ten days after His final words and ascension.

We cannot conclude, then, that they were not saved, nor that they were just waiting to be born again. Whether they were born again in the New Testament sense at this time is not a settled issue; however, that they were saved in the sense that, had they died, they would have gone into the presence of the Lord is clear.

Christ not only instructed them to wait, but gave them the reason: for the *"promise of the Father"* (Acts 1:4). Acts 2:1-4 then records the fulfillment of the promise.

Notice, Christ did not instruct them to wait for salvation or the new birth, but for an *"enduement"* (Luke 24:49) of power to be witnesses (Acts 1:8). As He later taught, those who were already His children should ask for the enduement of His Spirit. (Luke 11:13 -- by analogy, it was the children of God who should ask for the Spirit.)

* The Samaritans -- (Acts 8:1-14) -- Phillip preached Christ and saw many people converted and healed. He cast out devils and many received water baptism, yet they had not received the Holy Spirit. Peter and John later came down, laid hands on them, and they received the Spirit.

This gives clear, indisputable proof that the baptism in the Holy Spirit was a subsequent experience, distinct from salvation, and that, in fact, a definite lapse can occur.

NOTE: This incident took place about seven years after Pentecost.

* **Paul** -- (Acts 9:3-14) -- Paul experienced a marvelous and dramatic conversion on the Damascus Road. He prayed and sought God for the following three days. Yet he did not receive the Spirit until Ananias came and prayed for him.

* **The Ephesians** -- (Acts 19:1-7) -- Notice that verse 1 says that they were *"disciples."* Also, it is not recorded that Paul preached the Gospel to them as though their need was conversion, rather his inquiry to them was, *"Have ye received the Holy Ghost?"*

Translated literally, it does not say *"since,"* but rather, *"when ye believed."* By Paul's own declaration, they were believers who had been baptized in the past by John's baptism. Notice that even the form of Paul's question implies that a person could be a Christian without having received the Spirit. If the Spirit automatically fell on a person when he believed, then Paul would not have asked this question.

NOTE: This incident took place about twenty-one years after Pentecost.

A distinct experience by the witness of typology:

* **The feasts** -- The Feast of Passover speaks of the slain Lamb and His vicarious death for our redemption (Exodus 12; I Corinthians 5:7). Pentecost (day of first-fruits), which came fifty days later, speaks of the outpouring of the Spirit.

NOTE: Traditionally, the receiving of the law on Sinai corresponded with the first Pentecost. The Pentecost of Acts 2 brought spiritual fulfillment to this because it was then that God wrote the commandments on fleshy tables of men's hearts, rather than on stone.

When in the land of Canaan, the feast of Pentecost represented to Israel the celebrating of the first-fruits of the crops. This was also fulfilled initially in Acts 2:1-4 when God shed forth the first-fruits of the Spirit upon His people.

Pentecost requires an answer and a fulfillment in the believer's experience.

* **The blood and oil** -- (Exodus 29) -- For Aaron and his sons to become consecrated for the service of the sanctuary they were washed, clothed in holy garments, had blood applied to their right ear, thumb, and big toe, and immediately upon the fresh blood was placed the holy anointing oil. (God wants to fill believers when they accept the blood, not years later.) There was *oil* only where there was first *blood.*

The sprinkled blood is a type and agent of salvation, and the anointing of oil is a type of the anointing of the Holy Spirit (Luke 4:18). We see here two distinct truths in separate forms. (Other references referring to this anointing are: I John 2:20, 27; II Corinthians 1:21).

NOTE: Notice, in Aaron's case, the oil was poured on his head -- a type of Christ, our high priest, receiving a profusion of the Spirit; the anointing without measure (Psalm 133; John 3:34-35).

* **The baptism of the cloud and the sea** -- (I Corinthians 10:1-4) -- The nation Israel experienced both water and Spirit baptism in type. The crossing of the sea corresponds to water baptism, and the cloud corresponds to the baptism in the Spirit (heavenly baptism).

The New Testament links the water experience with the Spirit experience (John 3:5; Acts 10:44-47; I John 5:8).

NOTE: Both these experiences took place after the Passover lamb had been slain, which speaks of the blood of Christ for salvation. Note that God Himself was present in the cloud that guided Israel on their journey. The cloud took on two forms: by day a cloud of shade, comfort, and protection; by night a pillar of fire giving light and warmth. Remember that the Scripture calls the Spirit our *"Comforter"* and *"Guide."* In addition, the promised outpouring of the Spirit was said to involve *"fire"* (Matthew 3:11).

While we are sure that there are other typological evidences that could be presented, these three are prominent and unmistakably clear.

What is the Scriptural Evidence of the Baptism of the Spirit?

The pattern of the book of Acts:

Pentecost

Acts 2:4 -- *"And they were all filled with the Holy Ghost, and began to speak with other tongues, as the Spirit gave them utterance."*

In this passage, being filled with the Holy Spirit and speaking in tongues are indisputably connected. This is our purest example, in the sense that it was God's sovereign precedent; this was the way it happened initially; this was the way God introduced the experience into the church.

Samaria

Acts 8:15-19 -- *"Who, when they were come down, prayed for them, that they might receive the Holy Ghost: (For as yet He was fallen upon none of them: only they were baptized in the name of the Lord Jesus.) Then laid they their hands on them, and they received the Holy Ghost. And when Simon saw that through laying on of the apostles' hands the Holy Ghost was given, he offered them money, saying, Give me also this power, that on whomsoever I lay hands, he may receive the Holy Ghost."*

Though the word *"tongues"* is not mentioned in this passage, we notice that Simon saw the manifestation of the Spirit as the apostles laid hands on the people. He had already seen healings and casting out of devils, yet, he had not seen anything like what took place when the disciples received the Holy Ghost. We can only conclude that he saw the same manifestation which occurred in the other four Pentecostal experiences in the book of Acts.

Also, we might mention that Peter did not specifically mention tongues when reporting the incident at Cornelius' household to the Jews in Jerusalem (Acts 10:45-46). They understood that the baptism of the Holy Spirit and tongues were inseparable.

Paul

Acts 9:17 -- *"And Ananias went his way, and entered into the house; and putting his hands on him said, Brother Saul, the Lord, even Jesus, that appeared unto thee in the way as thou camest, hath sent me, that thou mightest receive thy sight, and be filled with the Holy Ghost."*

I Corinthians 14:18 -- *"I thank my God, I speak with tongues more than ye all."*

It is reasonable and Scripturally consistent to assume that Paul first spoke in tongues at the time he *"received the Spirit"* since other references confirm that this was God's pattern. We know that he did speak in tongues and that he did so profusely (I Corinthians 14:18).

Cornelius' household

Acts 10:45-46 -- *"And they of the circumcision which believe were astonished, as many as came with Peter, because that on the Gentiles also was poured out the gift of the Holy Ghost. For they heard them speak with tongues, and magnify God."*
Here again the *"gift of the Holy Ghost"* was evidenced by speaking in other tongues. The tongues were the sign to Peter and the Jews which caused them to know

unmistakably what it was that these Gentiles had received.

In Ephesus

Acts 19:2 -- *"He said unto them, Have ye received the Holy Ghost since ye believed? And they said unto him, We have not so much as heard whether there be any Holy Ghost."*

In verse six, he laid hands upon them and the Holy Ghost came on them and they *"spake with tongues, and prophesied."*

Again, tongues are connected with receiving the Spirit. Tongues became Scriptural evidence that one was filled with the Holy Ghost.

Often people have a very real visitation from the Holy Spirit which is to them a real "mountaintop experience," yet they do not yield to the Spirit with regards to speaking in tongues. They often insist that they have received the Spirit because of the reality and preciousness of the experience. This, of course, must be respected by all. Yet we must never establish any other or lesser evidence to be the sign of receiving the Holy Spirit than that which the Scriptures themselves teach. If such persons had yielded to the Spirit, they would have undoubtedly received His fullness for them, as receiving is definitely connected with responding and yielding. Therefore, they need to be taught to yield to the Spirit and allow Him to express Himself through their speech organs.

We might also observe that the tongues of fire or the rushing mighty wind that were seen and heard at Pentecost did not recur as a sign, but that tongues are the recurring sign and evidence of the baptism of the Spirit. It was because of the signs of tongues that the Jews knew that the household of Cornelius had received, for *"they heard them speak with tongues, and magnify God."*

It seems to be a principle with God in his dealings with man that spiritual realities and experiences have natural and physical manifestations in our lives. For example, when we have divine love, it shows itself by love for the brethren. Also, the thoughts of our hearts are expressed by our words. All the utterance gifts (I Corinthians 12) are manifested by the voice of the individual being used. Repentance is expressed by water baptism and public confession. And the receiving of the Spirit is manifested by speaking in tongues. It was *sense perceived*, not just as an invisible and mysterious operation of the Spirit in the human heart. It was both *seen* and *heard* (Acts 2:33; 10:45-46).

There is a difference between tongues as the initial evidence of the baptism in the Spirit and speaking in tongues as the *"gift of tongues."*

All the previous cases show that people spoke in tongues where they received the Spirit. In most cases, they did not abide in the Lord's instructions regarding how tongues were to be used to edify the assembly (I Corinthians 14). For example, they all spoke at once, I Corinthians 14:6, 23, 27 show this to be out of order in the assembly. Also, there was no interpretation, which I Corinthians 14:5, 28 show to be improper, as well, in the assembly.

We must remember that receiving the Spirit was not called the *"gift of tongues,"* but rather, the *"gift of the Holy Ghost,"* which included speaking in tongues. Scriptural precedent shows that all spoke in tongues upon receiving the Spirit. Paul shows that there is also a speaking in tongues among the various gifts given to the church for body ministry (I Corinthians 12:10,30; 14:5).

It was the confusing of these two, in fact, that the Lord sought to correct in the Corinthian church. Some came and spoke in tongues wholesale in the meetings, without any interpretation, producing abuses and confusion. So, through the Apostle Paul, the Lord sorted it out for them. He taught them that the assembly of God's people is to be respected and each person should seek to edify the body (I Corinthians 14:12); that messages in tongues given in the body be interpreted so all might benefit (14:5, 28).

Paul makes it clear, however, that he is not referring to their private use of tongues in prayer and praise to the Lord (14:4). He calls this *"praying in the Spirit"* and *"singing in the Spirit"* (vs. 15), and confirms the fact in other passages that we should practice it. For example, Ephesians 5:18-19 tell us to be full of the Spirit and speak to *"yourselves"* in spiritual singing. Ephesians 6:8 tells us to pray always *"in the Holy Spirit,"* and in Jude 20 we are told to build ourselves up by praying in the Holy Ghost. Paul, in fact, said he practiced speaking in tongues profusely, more than all the Corinthians put together (vs.18).

It must be remembered that in I Corinthians 14, Paul is writing to the Christians in Corinth concerning their conduct in the assembly and how to speak *"unto men"* (vs.2) by way of ministry and communication. He does not doom them to an unqualified silence of tongues, but rather, only silence *"in the church,"* except they be interpreted (vs.28). In fact, he uses the word church or churches nine times in this chapter; far more times than it is used in any other single chapter in the New Testament (vs. 4, 5, 12, 19, 23, 28, 33, 34, 35). In addition, notice the phrases *"when ye come together"* (vs. 26), and *"the whole church"* (vs. 23); remember that the context of this chapter is to teach us how to use tongues to the *"profit"* of the brethren (vs.6).

What are Scriptural reasons why believers speak in tongues?

* It is a sign that Christ is risen and glorified and seated in the heavens (Acts 2:33).

* It is a sign of personal acceptance of His Lordship (Acts 2:4, 32-39); total yieldedness, even to the point of yielding our most unruly member, the tongue (James 3:1-18).

* It is a sign that one has repented and received the Holy

Ghost. It is the initial sign of receiving the Holy Spirit (Acts 2:34, 38-39; 10:46-47; 19:6).

* It is to deal with human pride. To contact God, man must become childlike (I Corinthians 1:18-31; Matthew 18:2-5). It is a part of the "reproach" we bear (from the standpoint of the world and our human intellect.)

* That God might speak supernaturally to men (I Corinthians 12:10; 14:5, 13-22.)

* That men may speak to Gold supernaturally (I Corinthians 14:2, 16-18). This speaks of prayer and worship (I Corinthians 14:15-16; Acts 2:11; 10:45-46).

* To edify ourselves (I Corinthians 14:4, 15-16; Jude 20; Ephesians 6:18).

The soul and body unaided are not equipped with faculties for the complete expression of man's spirit. The newborn spirit communicates with the Lord through the newborn tongue (language). The language one's soul knows and the thought one's mind thinks, place great restrictions on the free expression of his spirit. One's spirit, indwelt by the Holy Spirit, transcends the soul and requires another means of expression other than that which the soul provides. That is why it is of great value not to limit one's prayers and worship to that which the mind comprehends. It is an advantage rather than a disadvantage not to know what one is saying. This by-passes the limited mental capacities and launches a person into the limitless realm of the Spirit of God.

Praying in tongues is a great key to the believer's walk in the Spirit. This was one of Paul's great secrets (I Corinthians 14:18).

Through giving ourselves to profusely using tongues in our private lives, the Holy Spirit continually empowers and energizes the whole man. Through this avenue God is able to give revelation and quickening to our minds and to infuse our whole emotional system with His Spirit; to continually influence our will to live in absolute obedience to Himself. Also through this avenue, physical health can be released and emerge from the life-giving Spirit within us, quickening our very bodies and thwarting the onslaughts of sickness and disease. This is why Paul, when placing restrictions and controls on tongues in the assembly, did just the opposite when referring to their private use. He encouraged the copious use of tongues. It is by this means we are able to rejuvenate and refresh the whole inner man (Isaiah 40:29-31).

Another aspect of building ourselves up through tongues is seen by a careful look at I Corinthians 14:5. It could validly read, *"I would that ye all speak in tongues in order that ye may prophesy..."* (a Greek hinaclause). Speaking in tongues, in other words, is a building block that leads to interpretation and prophecy. This verse is not contrasting two things, but speaking of a progression. Speaking and singing in tongues is the easiest and most uncomplicated way of learning to prophesy.

* To be a sign to the unbeliever (I Corinthians 14:22).

* To fulfill Bible prophecy (Isaiah 28:11).

* It is a sign to the believer (Mark 16:17; Acts 11:45-46; John 7:38-39; Acts 1:8).

What is it that tongues seem to attract more attention and discussion than the other gifts?

* Because opponents make an issue of it. This forces those who believe in tongues to talk about it. Often that is all Pentecostals seem to talk about because that is all they are asked about.

* Because often those who speak in tongues have over-emphasized it in their teaching and practice. This has

often been done in a carnal and defensive way, thus becoming unnecessarily offensive.

* Because they have been used out of scriptural order in church meetings: not having interpretations, by having an excessive number of messages in tongues, etc.

* Because by its very nature, it is a supernatural sign or manifestation that attracts much attention.

* Because tongues are the potential common possession of every believer and should, therefore, be very prevalent. They are, therefore, likely to be greatly noticeable, especially if abused.

* Tongues are often used as the basis for criticism by scoffers, unbelievers and the uninitiated. It is a sign that causes offense to those whose hearts are not open to God.

* Because it is being restored. The fact of its historic neglect and absence now accents its being widely manifested as God pours out His Spirit on all flesh.

Often in the process of restoring a lost facet of truth, that truth will be over-emphasized. This is almost required in order for that truth to be maneuvered back into its proper place of balance, just as a person with a severe lack of a certain vitamin must often be prescribed massive doses for a short time until his system is in proper balance.

Is it the Holy Spirit who speaks or is it me?

In a sense, it is both, but it helps our understanding most to realize that we must speak. We use our own speech organs by the act of our own wills cooperating with the Spirit who is prompting us.

Acts 2:4 -- *"And they were all filled with the Holy Ghost, and began to speak."* (Notice, *"they"* did the speaking.)

I Corinthians 14:15 -- *"I will pray...with the Spirit."*
"I will sing...with the Spirit."

It is not accurate to say that the Holy Spirit speaks in tongues. He quickens you and you speak in tongues. Yet in a general way, it is proper to say the Spirit is speaking through us. This principle is illustrated in the following references.

Acts 13:2 -- *"The Holy Ghost said..."* (probably through one of the prophets present).

I Timothy 4:1 -- *The Spirit speaketh expressly..."* (yet it was through Paul that the message actually came).

The Spirit is the source of motivation, yet I must obey and cooperate without expecting Him to overwhelm or overpower me. I do it while I am still fully conscious and have voluntary possession of senses.

Is it proper for believers to pray or worship in tongues together at the same time?

Paul's instructions in I Corinthians 14 gives us the order for most of our general assemblies. If, however, a believer's meeting were held just for the purpose of corporate prayer, this presents a little different picture. Where the meeting is an established believer's meeting, there is perhaps greater liberty than when unbelievers are present. It is our conviction that in a meeting such as this, where the entire emphasis is on communicating to God and not each other, that corporate prayer and praise in tongues is in order. There is, in fact, great power and blessing in it.

We know that the early church prayed as a group (Luke 24:52-53; Acts 4:24-31; Acts 12:12,21; 23:2) and that on several occasions, they all spoke in tongues corporately (Acts 2:1-4; 10:45-46; 19:6).

There are many times when God leads His people to sing

or speak together in the Spirit. There have been waves of this down through history as well as in our day. Often in revival, it just breaks out sovereignly as God moves upon a group of people.

The main issue is that such praise and worship should not produce confusion or disharmony, but should be done unitedly and with the sole purpose of worshipping God or praying. The main issue is largely, with whom are we purposing to communicate, God or man?

10

What are the Purposes of the Baptism of the Holy Spirit?

It must be remembered that Jesus said much more about the promise of the Father (Acts 1:4) than is recorded in Acts 1:8. When He said we would receive power to be *"witnesses unto Me,"* it was really a very broad statement and did not give details as to how it would be worked out, since to be witnesses for Christ involves our total lives. It was really an all inclusive summary of the Spirit's ministry.

The purpose of believers receiving the Spirit has many aspects to it, but can be summarized as receiving *"power"*: being power-packed witnesses on earth for the Lord. This not only involved our verbal testimony, but a quality of life which produces the visible testimony Jesus speaks of in Matthew 5:16, *"Let your light so shine before men, that they may see your good works, and glorify your Father which is in heaven."* Even the phrases *"filled with"* or *"baptized with"* the Spirit are general in our understanding until we combine all the Scriptural references which teach specific facets of what these experiences involve.

The Scripture emphasizes this experience on a broader, more permanent and continuous scale than is usually understood. The emphasis has often been strong on the initial act of receiving the Spirit, but weak on the continuous effects it is to have on our lives. Receiving the promise of the Father and being *"filled"* with the Spirit speaks of the invasion of our total life and walk by the Spirit of God. It means being immersed in, or plunged into, the realm of the Spirit. By divorcing the *initial* from the *continual,* we cause people to stop short. By stressing the beginning of the journey and not the journey itself, we have a wrong focus, which produces a wrong emphasis in our practical lives.

This is the way the Apostle Paul treated divine truths. In Romans 6, when speaking of conversion using the analogy and in the language of water baptism, he showed the effect that experience was to have on the entire walk and the life of the believer (Romans 6:1-18). This same treatment appears over and over in his writings. In fact, one of Paul's greatest emphases throughout his writings is summarized by Galatians 5:25, *"If we live in the Spirit, let us also walk in the Spirit."* In other words, it is not enough to get into the realm or sphere of the Spirit. We must continually walk under the Spirit's influence.

The underlying message of the baptism of the Spirit is that its purpose is power and spiritual enablement. In the Old Testament, the anointing oil prepared each priest for priestly service. Christ received this prior to His ministry in the dove experience at Jordan. The oil speaks to us strongly of qualifying and empowering for ministry. No Old Testament priest dared try to minister without this enabling.

Similarly, this power from the Holy Spirit has two aspects: the oil, both saturated and emanated; there is to be absorption and radiation, charge and discharge. That is, both affects the person's inner life and produces an effect and response on the part of those to whom he ministers. It changes the person into the character of Christ, and draws others to Christ.

We are both *baptized in* (submerged) and *filled with* the Spirit. Being filled implies that we actually contain Him. The Spirit not only surrounds us as water does when being baptized, but He fills us. He both saturates our exteriors and floods our interiors; not only waters to swim in, but waters flowing out of the belly (Ezekiel 47; John 7:38).

Let us list the major aspects which the Scriptures reveal as God's purposes in giving us the *"promise of the Father."*

It brings power for the operation of the gifts of the Spirit:

I Corinthians 12:1-12 -- *"Now concerning spiritual gifts, brethren, I would not have you ignorant. Ye know that ye were Gentiles, carried away unto these dumb idols, even as ye were led. Wherefore I give you to understand, that no man speaking by the Spirit of God calleth Jesus accursed: and that no man can say that Jesus is Lord, but by the Holy Ghost. Now there are diversities of gifts, but the same Spirit. And there are differences of administrations, but the same Lord. And there are diversities of operations, but it is the same God which worketh all in all. But the manifestation of the Spirit is given to every man to profit withal. For to one is given by the Spirit the word of wisdom; to another the word of knowledge by the same Spirit; to another faith by the same Spirit; to another gifts of healing by the same Spirit; to another the working of miracles; to another prophecy; to another discerning of spirits; to another divers kinds of tongues; to another the interpretation of tongues: But all these worketh that one and the selfsame Spirit, dividing to every man severally as He will. For as the body is one, and hath many members, and all the members of that one body, being many, are one body: so also is Christ."*

These are not just human talents. The operation of these gifts requires the direct activity and influence of the Holy Spirit (I Corinthians 12:7). They have to do primarily with ministry to the body, or the believer's ministry in the church. They are tools designed to build up (edify) the body of Christ (I Corinthians 14:12).

The gifts also enable the local group of believers to form a spiritual body, manifesting the complete ministry of Christ in a given area. The body of Christ is not only designed as a body to meet the needs of its organs, but to present Christ in fullness to the community.

It is the baptism in the Holy Ghost and "fire":

Matthew 3:11-12 -- *"I indeed baptize you with water unto repentance: but He that cometh after me is mightier than I, whose shoes I am not worthy to bear: He shall baptize you with the Holy Ghost and with fire: Whose fan is in His hand, and He will thoroughly purge His floor, and gather His wheat into the garner; but He will burn up the chaff with unquenchable fire."*

We saw in Chapter 3 that He was called the *"Spirit of burning."* Fire is used for many purposes, but the fire itself consumes and refines, as is the emphasis of verse 12. There are areas in the believer's life which the Spirit consumes at conversion, and it is also a continuing activity in the life of the believer. Salvation involves a death as well as a birth (Romans 6:3; 7:4) and Romans 8:13 tells us we are to continue to put to death *("mortify")* the deeds of the flesh by the power of the Spirit.

11

How Does a Person Receive the Baptism in the Holy Spirit?

The general conditions necessary:

Very simply, if one is going to be baptized with the Spirit they must have experienced the new birth. Therefore, true repentance and a confession of faith in Christ as Lord is a pre-requisite to receiving the baptism of the Spirit.

Acts 2:38 -- *"Then Peter said unto them, Repent, and be baptized every one of you in the name of Jesus Christ for the remission of sins, and ye shall receive the gift of the Holy Ghost."*

The response of faith:

Galatians 3:2 -- *"This only would I learn of you, Received ye the Spirit by the works of the law, or by the hearing of faith?"*

Faith is the condition upon which man receives everything from God (Hebrews 11:6; James 1:6-8).

The tendency of man is to lean on senses and emotions. Therefore, if he does not have *sense righteousness*, or feel worthy, he closes himself off from the blessings of God.

It is of great importance to notice the word *"gift"* in Acts 2:38. God specified that it was to be a gift given, not purchased. One doesn't buy a gift; he simply receives it.

Repentance and the new birth prepare a person to be filled

with the Spirit, not works or merit or Christian character and maturity. If God births, He will fill. We can only receive God's gifts by faith, the same way we were saved. It is this faith condition which is the prerequisite for salvation, for being filled with the Spirit, for healing, to operate gifts, etc.

It is not necessary to teach people to *"tarry"* for the Spirit. The believers in the early church did not teach or practice this. However, we may make a waiting period necessary through unbelief or by trying to become worthy before receiving. One of the greatest lessons we learn, however, if we do tarry, is that it is unnecessary. Long waiting is not a virtue but rather a frustration to the individual as well as to the grace of God (Galatians 2:21). The amount of time one waits will depend on his faith and obedience.

Those who were saved under a "partial gospel":

To those believers who were not properly taught and therefore did not receive the baptism of the Spirit at conversion (or soon after), the following instructions become necessary:

* **That it is Biblical** -- It is a valid Biblical experience and is both applicable to and necessary for our day. (This is covered in Chapters 8, 9, 14.)

   Romans 10:17 -- *"So then faith cometh by hearing, and hearing by the word of God."*

   This shows that the Word must first be sown in order to have faith.

   Ephesians 5:17-18 -- *"Wherefore be ye not unwise, but understanding what the will of the Lord is. And be not drunk with wine, wherein is excess; but be filled with the Spirit."*

   This shows that it is not an option, rather a command to

be filled with the Spirit.

* **That it is an experience distinct from repentance and water baptism** -- (and the new birth, covered in Chapter 8).

* **That it is evidenced by speaking in tongues** -- (covered in Chapter 9).

If a person is not convinced concerning these areas, then the foundation of God's Word is not fully laid. That then must be the goal. It is the sad truth that, regarding this subject, the *"traditions of men"* have made the Word of God of *"none effect"* for millions of believers (Mark 7:13). It is often necessary to deal with these traditions in the light of pure Scripture.

* **That there must be heart preparation** -- The next thing one should do is to prepare his heart to receive by hungering and seeking and asking for the Holy Spirit. This means we cannot take a neutral position, expecting God to seek us and sovereignly pour out His Spirit on us.

Luke 11:9-13 -- *"And I say unto you, Ask, and it shall be given you; seek, and ye shall find; knock, and it shall be opened unto you. For every one that asketh receiveth; and he that seeketh findeth; and to him that knocketh it shall be opened. If a son shall ask bread of any of you that is a father, will he give him a stone? or if he ask a fish, will he for a fish give him a serpent? Or if he shall ask an egg, will he offer him a scorpion? If ye then, being evil, know how to give good gifts unto your children: how much more shall your heavenly Father give the Holy Spirit to them that ask him?"*
Jesus instructs us to ask, seek and knock when desiring to receive the Spirit.

Matthew 5:6 -- *"Blessed are they which do hunger and thirst after righteousness: for they shall be filled."*

Here we see the same principle brought out. To receive any spiritual blessing or experience from the Lord, we must desire it and seek after it.

(See also James 4:8-10 -- it shows the importance of taking the initiative in order to receive from God.)

One aspect of seeking would be to have the elders and other believers lay hands on and pray for the filling with the Spirit. This was done on several occasions in Scripture (Acts 8:17; 19:6).

* **That he must then respond in faith and obedience to receive the Spirit** -- It is both a supernatural and natural experience; it is the moving of the Holy Spirit combined with human yielding, response and faith.

The miracle is not so much *that* the person is speaking as it is *what* he is speaking. The Spirit gave them utterance on the day of Pentecost, and *they spoke* (Acts 2:4). The words are not a product of one's mind, rather they come from his spirit (John 7:38-39).

The truth of the cooperative action between man and God is illustrated in several places.

Matthew 10:19-20 -- *"But when they deliver you up, take no thought how or what ye shall speak: for it shall be given you in that same hour what ye shall speak. For it is not ye that speak, but the Spirit of your Father which speaketh in you."*

"...ye shall speak..."

"...the Spirit...speaketh in you..."

I Corinthians 14:15 -- *"What is it then? I will pray with the Spirit, and I will pray with the understanding also: I will sing with the Spirit, and I will sing with the understanding also."*

"...I will pray...with the Spirit..."

I Corinthians 3:9 -- *"For we are laborers together with God: ye are God's husbandry, ye are God's building."*

"...we are laborers...with God..."

It is more than thirsting, it is drinking; it is more than asking, it is actively receiving; it is not only offered as a gift, it must be taken. Someone aptly put it this way: "Prayer is asking for rain; faith is carrying an umbrella."

Other remarks and helps:

* Remember, we must seek the Lord, not just an experience. We must also be willing to yield to the leading of the Spirit, even regarding speaking in tongues.

* We need not fear receiving something evil or less than God's promise when we come to God as a born-again child, and as a hungry, honest seeker after the Spirit (Luke 11:11-13).

* We should not attempt to work up our emotions or *"work down"* a blessing, rather yield to the Lord and relax in His presence. (This is the principle of Romans 10:6-8.)

* The principle of Psalm 22:3 should be remembered: *"Thou art holy, O thou that inhabitest the praises of Israel."* An atmosphere of worship is that which always brings the presence of God. Therefore, we should worship God freely and without reservation. Those who refuse to open their mouths seldom receive, because this experience has to do with the mouth and voice. (Combine Luke 24:52-53 with Acts 2:1.)

* Once we have been filled, speaking in tongues daily is a key to spiritual vitality and growth.

Jude 20 -- *"But ye, beloved, building up yourselves on your most holy faith, praying the Holy Ghost."*

I Corinthians 14:4 -- *"He that speaketh in an unknown tongue edifieth himself."*

I Corinthians 14:18 -- *"I thank my God, I speak with tongues more than ye all."*

* It should also be remembered that the degree of our hunger and thirst determines the depth of our experience (Psalm 42:1-2; Matthew 5:6).

* There may be a period of waiting on God and seeking the infilling. This is never time wasted. It may involve frustration, which is not to be looked upon as a sign that it is not of God or not for the seeker. One must instead look upon himself as being *enroute* to the proper ripeness, understanding and faith to receive. Hunger is not always a pleasant experience, but the appetite is necessary to the partaking.

* It must be remembered that this experience is not an end, but a beginning. It is not the completion, but the commencement into the realms of the Spirit. It is not as much a goal as it is a door.

12

What is the Relationship of the Holy Spirit to a Believer who has not been Filled with the Spirit?

To our knowledge, there are three major views on this theme held by believers. We will briefly present each view with the evidences used to support it.

The varying degree of measure view:

Degree of measure view holds that every believer has the Spirit abiding within him, but not in the same measure of anointing and power as one who is baptized in the Spirit.

Romans 8:9 -- *"But ye are not in the flesh, but in the Spirit, if so be that the Spirit of God dwell in you. Now if any man have not the Spirit of Christ, he is none of His."*

This reference shows that everyone converted has received the Spirit (a measure) yet the baptism or filling of the Spirit has to do with rivers of living water of which Christ spoke in John 7:37-38.

I Corinthians 12:3 -- *"...no man can say that Jesus is the Lord, but by the Holy Ghost."*

This shows the inseparableness of confessing Christ as Lord and the presence of the Holy Spirit.

Romans 8:15-16 -- *"For ye have not received the spirit of bondage again to fear; but ye have received the Spirit of adoption, whereby we cry, Abba, Father. The Spirit itself beareth witness with our spirit, that we are the children of*

God."

This speaks of the adoption of sons and the in-dwelling Spirit as being inseparable. Therefore, any believer, in order to be a son, must have the Spirit. (See also Galatians 4:6; I John 3:24; 4:13.)

Titus 3:5 -- *"Not by works of righteousness which we have done, but according to His mercy He saved us, by the washing of regeneration, and renewing of the Holy Ghost."*

Connecting regeneration and the operation of the Holy Spirit, therefore, in order to be regenerated one must have the Spirit.

Everyone saved is *"in"* the Spirit, yet not necessarily *"filled"* with or walking in the Spirit (Galatians 5:25; Ephesians 5:18 -- both written to believers). This is illustrated by the Samaritans (Acts 8) and the Ephesians (Acts 19).

In addition to the new birth operation of the Spirit, there is another, which has as its special purpose, energizing men for the service of God and having Him manifest Himself through men in powerful ways through the *"gifts."* The gifts are said to be *"manifestations of the Spirit,"* not just human talent (I Corinthians 12:7-10). The Spirit not only has His deep inner work, but produces outward, supernatural manifestations in the believer's life.

The "with" but not "in" view:

This view holds that every born-again believer has the presence of the Spirit *"with,"* but not actually dwelling in him. The Spirit performs the new birth and regeneration, yet does not abide within.

The headquarters passage for this view is found in John 14:16-17 -- *"And I will pray the Father, and He shall give you another Comforter, that He may abide with you for ever; even the Spirit of truth; whom the world cannot receive, because it*

*seeth Him not, neither knoweth Him: but ye know Him; for
He dwelleth with you, and shall be in you."*

It is concluded from this passage that the Spirit was *"with"*
the disciples before the infilling, but *"in"* them after (the
infilling being in Acts 2).

Acts 19:2 -- *"He said unto them, Have ye received the Holy
Ghost since ye believed? And they said unto him, We have
not so much as heard whether there be any Holy Ghost."*

This passage, according to this view, shows that one can be
a believer without having received the Holy Ghost. It is
concluded, then, that if a person has not received the Holy
Ghost, then He does not abide in him.

The objection to this view is that it tells some believers that
they are not indwelt by the Holy Spirit, which robs them of
a vital and precious part of their faith. It could, in fact,
show doubt in many concerning the reality of their salvation
if they feel they do not have the Spirit indwelling in them.
It also causes many to oppose the *"Pentecostal"* believers
because it says, in essence, that if you do not speak in
tongues, then you must not be saved.

The "in" but not "upon" view:

This view holds that every born-again Christian has the
Spirit within him in the sense of indwelling and abiding, yet
he has not necessarily received the *"upon"* ministry of the
Spirit that imparts power for service.

To present this view, let us look at the words *"within"* and
"upon," which emphasize two aspects of the ministry of the
Spirit.

* **The "within" or indwelling ministry of the Spirit** -- This
is in connection with salvation and sonship.

   Romans 8:9-10 -- *"But ye are not in the flesh, but in the*

Spirit, if so be that the Spirit of God dwell in you. Now if any man have not the Spirit of Christ, he is none of His. And if Christ be in you, the body is dead because of sin; but the Spirit is life because of righteousness."

John 14:17 -- *"Even the Spirit of truth; whom the world cannot receive, because it seeth Him not, neither knoweth Him: but ye know Him; for He dwelleth with you, and shall be in you."*

It was the *"with"* or *"in"* ministry of the Spirit which the apostles experienced in their ministry prior to the crucifixion and their new birth.

Ephesians 3:17 -- *"That Christ may dwell in your hearts by faith; that ye, being rooted and grounded in love..."*

"Dwell" as used here is "to inhabit or reside in."

(See also Galatians 4:6; Romans 8:15; I John 5:12; I Corinthians 3:16; Ezekiel 11:19.)

Every believer has Christ dwelling within him. This is synonymous with having *"life,"* or being born again.

Every believer can yield to the indwelling Spirit for a measure of victory to live the Christian life and to produce the fruit of the Spirit in his life (Galatians 5:22-23). In fact, I Corinthians 2:11-12 shows that every believer can have revelation from the Word and a level of understanding in the things of God. Acts 8:8 shows that Christians can have great joy at conversion and still not be baptized in the Spirit.

Therefore, none of these above conditions are evidence that one is filled with the Spirit or that baptism in the Holy Spirit is not necessary.

* **The *"upon"* ministry of the Spirit** -- The Greek word for *"upon"* is *epi.* It means "to be enveloped; to be completely covered or clothed in."

A key factor here is that, where the New Testament mentions it and where it is promised in the Old Testament, the baptism of the Spirit is spoken of as being *"upon."*

Joel 2:28 -- *"And it shall come to pass afterward, that I will pour out My Spirit upon all flesh; and your sons and your daughters shall prophesy, your old men shall dream dreams, your young men shall see visions."*

Luke 24:49 -- *"And, behold, I send the promise of My Father upon you: but tarry ye in the city of Jerusalem, until ye be endued with power from on high."*

Acts 1:8 -- *"But ye shall receive power, after that the Holy Ghost is come upon you: and ye shall be witnesses unto Me both in Jerusalem, and in all Judea, and Samaria, and unto the uttermost part of the earth."*

Acts 8:16 -- *"(For as yet He was fallen upon none of them: only they were baptized in the name of the Lord Jesus.)"*

NOTE: They already had *"within"* or indwelling ministry. They were already saved and water baptized.

Acts 10:44 -- *"While Peter yet spake these words, the Holy Ghost fell on all them which heard the Word."*

In the interlinear Greek: *"...fell the Spirit of the Holy upon..."*

Acts 11:15 -- *"And as I began to speak, the Holy Ghost fell on them, as on us at the beginning."*

Greek reads: *"...fell the Spirit of the Holy upon..."*

Acts 19:6 -- *"And when Paul had laid his hands upon them, the Holy Ghost came on them; and they spake with tongues, and prophesied."*

Greek: *"...came the Spirit of the Holy upon them..."*

NOTE: This happened after they had been baptized in
water and had the Spirit indwelling them.

So we see a pattern form: the Spirit's coming, the
baptism for empowering was spoken of as His *"upon"*
ministry.

(See also Acts 2:3; Numbers 11:25-29; 24:2; Judges 3:10;
6.34, 11.29, 14:6,19; 15:14.)

God's acts of power manifested through men in the Old
Testament were in connection with the Spirit coming
"upon" them.

We should note that the New Testament takes for granted
that every believer who follows the command of Jesus
(Mark 16:17) and the Word of God received the baptism of
the Spirit (Acts 2:38-39). The norm in the early church was
that all who were exposed to the Gospel were filled with the
Spirit. So the Bible does not offer great defenses on the
question, *"Do I have to receive the Holy Spirit and speak with
tongues?"*

13

What are the Offenses Committed Against the Spirit?

Resisting the Spirit:

Acts 7:51 -- *"Ye stiffnecked and uncircumcised in heart and ears, ye do always resist the Holy Ghost: as your fathers did, so do ye."*

This speaks of opposing and striving against the Lord. Stephen calls the Jews *"stiffnecked,"* not having a heart to obey God or hear His Word. This sin, therefore, involves stubbornness and open disobedience; openly refusing instruction and the Word of the Lord.

II Timothy 3:8 -- *"Now as Jannes and Jambres withstood Moses, so do these also resist the truth: men of corrupt minds, reprobate concerning the faith."*

(See also Exodus 32:9; I Samuel 8:19; II Chronicles 24:19; Jeremiah 32:33; 44:16; Zechariah 7:11.)

Grieving the Spirit:

Ephesians 4:30 -- *"And grieve not the Holy Spirit of God, whereby ye are sealed unto the day of temptation."*

(See also Psalm 78:40.)

Grief is a deep sadness or sorrow. It speaks of intense and inner affliction. Notice in Jeremiah 45:3, *"for the Lord hath added grief to my sorrow."* This suggests the severity of the experience of grief. It goes beyond just sorrow.

The Holy Spirit is a dove and is very sensitive. All bitterness, anger, resentment, quarreling, abusive and evil speech, lying one to another, giving place to the devil, stealing, etc., are a grief to Him (Ephesians 4:25-29).

Isaiah 63:10 -- *"But they rebelled and vexed His Holy Spirit: therefore He was turned to be their enemy, and He fought against them."*

(Also see Genesis 6:6; Psalm 95:9-10.)

Lying to the Spirit:

Acts 5:3-4 -- *"But Peter said, Ananias, why hath Satan filled thine heart to lie to the Holy Ghost, and to keep back part of the price of the land? While it remained, was it not thine own? and after it was sold, was it not in thine own power? why hast thou conceived this thing in thine heart? thou hast not lied unto men, but unto God."*

Notice, lying to the Lord (Spirit) was done by lying to the ministry. Ananias and his wife yielded to the suggestion of evil spirits to deceive God's servants, thus classifying themselves among those who *"speak lies in hypocrisy"* (I Timothy 4:2).

(See Psalm 62:4.)

Quenching the Spirit:

I Thessalonians 5:19 -- *"Quench not the Spirit."*

Quench means to "extinguish, smother, or put out." Thus this has to do with the failure to obey and respond to something the Spirit prompts a person to do, whether prophesying and manifesting spiritual gifts, witnessing to another about Christ, or obeying His dictates in Christian living. It means to quench or smother the Spirit's will. Churches can do this by forbidding prophecy and the expression of the gifts (I Thessalonians 5:20). Individuals can do it by being fearful and apprehensive, not responding to what the Spirit prompts them to do.

The step that comes after quenching the Spirit would be grieving Him. If we persist to quench the Spirit's operation and leading, we will grieve Him.

Blaspheming the Holy Spirit:

Matthew 12:31-32 -- *"Wherefore I say unto you, All manner of sin and blasphemy shall be forgiven unto men: but the blasphemy against the Holy Ghost shall not be forgiven unto men. And whosoever speaketh a word against the Son of man, it shall be forgiven him: but whosoever speaketh against the Holy Ghost, it shall not be forgiven him, neither in this world, neither in the world to come."*

To blaspheme means "to speak abusively of, to rail or speak contempt against God or things sacred." It is important to keep the term in its Scriptural context and not throw it around loosely.

Israel continued to be a rebellious and stiff-necked people, rejecting and resisting Christ at every possible opportunity. They were filling up the *"measure"* of their fathers' iniquity (Matthew 23:32). They were hardhearted and cruel, even in the face of Christ's miracles of deliverance and compassion (Matthew 12:22-30). They not only rejected Jesus as a man, but also the power of the Holy Ghost working through Him.

This is especially serious when we realize that Christ's miracles were done by the Spirit and were designed to testify of who He was. The Spirit confirmed or sealed Christ's message by divine acts of healings, etc. (John 5:36; 10:36-38). Christ ties in this truth in Matthew 12:28. He was doing His works by the Spirit, to seal His identity and the fact that what He was doing was part of the kingdom of God.

To reject His works and attribute them to demons was the sin of the Pharisees. They recognized His power, and they did not deny it or call Him a hoax or a phony. Instead they actually took the worst possible position, attributing it to Beelzebub (connected with Baal, the god of Ekron -- II Kings 1:2).

Their accusation constituted a final and persistent rejection of the Spirit's testimony of Christ. It was not a single act but a continuous resisting of the Spirit. It was not out of ignorance or without spiritual awareness that they spoke, but outright refusal and rejection of all divine testimony. They, in fact, made the occasion of the displayed power of the Spirit an opportunity to show spite towards Christ, the Son of God. Such people are without hope and bear the unmistakable stamp of perdition. This was the sin into which many of the Israelites fell.

This sin then constitutes a rejection of Christ following the Holy Spirit's revelation of who He is; it is to knowingly slander and refuse Him. This point of revelation is not just at hearing a sermon or a Sunday School lesson. Rather, it is after the Spirit bears unmistakable and powerful witness of Christ. Even Jesus, who had preached many times and lived among them said, *"Forgive them, for they know not..."* (Luke 23:34).

This spiritual revelation of who He is as in Matthew 16:16, *"Thou art the Christ, the Son of the living God,"* is a point of illumination, not just information; at which a person might receive Christ as Savior, but instead, rejects Him and blasphemes that revelation.

14

What are the Purposes of the Gifts of the Spirit and are They for Today?

Each of the nine gifts listed in I Corinthians 12:7-10 will be explained and dealt with individually in later chapters. It should be understood, however, that they are not just human talents, or even human abilities energized by the Holy Spirit. The gifts are direct manifestations of the Holy Spirit through believers. God does use human abilities and He does energize them with His Spirit, but that is something different than the gifts of the Spirit. It may also be true that God equips us by personality and temperament to match the gifts in which we function, yet the actual function of the gifts is beyond the personality and ability of the man, they function by the supernatural influence and operation of the Holy Spirit.

The purpose of the gifts:

* "To profit withal"

I Corinthians 12:7 -- *"But the manifestation of the Spirit is given to every man to profit withal."*

"Withal" here means for everyone, or for the common good of all. God does not give gifts to an individual for his own benefit, but to benefit the body of which he is a member. (We have already discussed the difference between tongues as a gift and tongues as the general evidence of receiving the Spirit and their use in personal edification in Chapter 9.)

I Corinthians 14:12 -- *"Even so ye, forasmuch as ye are zealous of spiritual gifts, seek that ye may excel to the edifying of the church."*

Ephesians 4:16 -- *"From whom the whole body fitly joined together and compacted by that which every joint supplieth, according to the effectual working in the measure of every part, maketh increase of the body unto the edifying of itself in love."*

This verse shows the responsibility every organ has to add to the growth of the body. Gifts are the tools or the means provided by Christ, whereby the church (the body) might mature and become a full grown *"man"* (Ephesians 4:13-15).

* **"To form a body"**

I Corinthians 12:27 -- *"Now ye are the body of Christ, and members in particular."*

The whole of I Corinthians 12 uses the analogy of a human body. The word *"body"* is used 18 times in this chapter--more than all other references to the word body (where the word body refers to the believers in the church) in the rest of the New Testament.

The body of Christ is not just a gathering of believers. The way to form a local body is to have organs that properly relate to each other and function in the gifts of the Spirit. Even where two or three gather and Christ is there in their midst, it is not a complete body. The presence of the Lord alone among people does not automatically make that gathering a body. If we insist on calling it a body, the best we can say is that it is a paralyzed and crippled one if these gifts do not function.

Of course, these nine gifts of the Spirit are not the totality of body ministry, but total body ministry is not possible without them. A local church can only produce the fruit for which Christ is working through body ministry.

Notice in Romans 12 where Scripture also speaks about the gifts, it again ties in the theme of the body (vs. 4-5). This is true of I Corinthians 14 as well, which speaks of the operations of tongues, interpretation and prophecy. The context in this passage is the church, or the body. The word *"church"* is used nine times in this chapter.

So we see the pattern: when God talks about gifts, He also talks about bodies or local churches. It is not Scriptural to practice the gifts without being connected to a local body of believers, where there is edification within the safety of body ministry, and under proven oversight.

Are the gifts necessary for our day?

On the basis of what we have just read, we must say that the gifts are still needed, both for the edification of the church and that the body of Christ might be formed. The argument that the supernatural was needed only in the primitive church is man's misunderstanding; we find no hint of such a doctrine in Scripture. In addition, a far greater need for the supernatural manifestations of the Spirit exists now than ever before in the history of the world, particularly in view of the soon-coming Lord and the great harvest that is to be reaped prior to that time.

Supernatural gifts were said by Christ to be the *"credentials"* of the believer.

Mark 16:17-20 -- *"And these signs shall follow them that believe; In My name shall they cast out devils; they shall speak with new tongues; they shall take up serpents; and if they drink any deadly thing, it shall not hurt them; they shall lay hands on the sick, and they shall recover. So then after the Lord had spoken unto them, He was received up into heaven, and sat on the right hand of God. And they went forth, and preached every where, the Lord working with them, and confirming the word with signs following. Amen."*

The Gospel needs to have *"signs following,"* to be fully and effectively preached. This fact can be verified by the following Scripture references, as well as many others.

Romans 15:17-20 -- *"I have therefore whereof I may glory through Jesus Christ in those things which pertain to God. For I will not dare to speak of any of those things which Christ hath not wrought by me, to make the Gentiles obedient, by word and deed, through mighty signs and wonders, by the power of the Spirit of God; so that from Jerusalem, and round about unto Illyricum, I have fully preached the gospel of Christ. Yea, so have I strived to preach the gospel, not where Christ was named, lest I should build upon another man's foundation."*

I Corinthians 2:4 -- *"And my speech and my preaching was not with enticing words of man's wisdom, but in demonstration of the Spirit and of power."*

Acts 8:6 -- *"And the people with one accord gave heed unto those things which Philip spake, hearing and seeing the miracles which he did."*

Hebrews 2:4 -- *"God also bearing them witness, both with signs and wonders, and with divers miracles, and gifts of the Holy Ghost, according to His own will."*

The gifts of the Spirit are vital to the body of Christ (believers) and to the local church body. The gifts are the tools for the body to use to bring growth and maturation in Christ, and the fulfillment of the Word for the New Testament church.

Ephesians 4:11-13 -- *"And he gave some apostles; and some, prophets; and some, evangelists; and some, pastors and teachers; for the perfecting of the saints, for the work of the ministry, for the edifying of the body of Christ: till we all come in the unity of the faith, and of the knowledge of the Son of God, unto a perfect man, unto the measure of the stature of the fulness of Christ."*

Other thoughts on the gifts of the Spirit:

The question may arise, *"Does each believer have all nine of the gifts?"* To answer this, read carefully I Corinthians 12:4-11 and Ephesians 4:16.

The obvious implication of the Scripture is that no man is complete in himself; we absolutely need each other. An individual is only one member or organ of the body of Christ, regardless of how *"gifted"* he may be. Collectively, we make up the body of Christ as a local church. (I Corinthians 12:27 -- *"Now ye are the body of Christ, and members in particular."*)

God may choose to manifest Himself through a single individual with all nine of the gifts, scattered throughout the New Testament. This, however, does not mean that all nine of the gifts took place in every local church where that person ministered. Here we have listed the references that speak of Paul being used through many of the gifts:

Gift of the word of wisdom -- II Peter 3:15
Gift of knowledge -- Acts 13:11
Gift of discerning of spirits -- Acts 16:6-18
Gift of tongues -- I Corinthians 14:18
Gift of interpretation -- I Corinthians 14:13
Gift of prophecy -- I Corinthians 14:6
Gift of faith -- Romans 15:18-21
Gift of healing -- Acts 14:8-10
Gift of miracles -- Acts 20:9-12

We realize more could be added to this list, and that some of these are built on what might be called an *obvious inference*. How could Paul, for example, write all the inspired and infallible instructions on the use and function of all the gifts if he did not have firsthand experience? We must remember that Paul was an apostle whose charge it was to write more of the New Testament than any other writer.

To summarize this, we would like to mention five strong

thoughts which should affect every person's attitude toward the gifts:

* Every believer is to have at least one manifestation of the Spirit functioning in his life (I Corinthians 12:7).

* We are not to be ignorant of our gifts (I Corinthians 12:1-6; I Peter 4:10).

* We are not to neglect our gifts (I Timothy 4:14). But we are to stir them up (II Timothy 1:6-7).

* We are to desire strongly to have gifts that edify (I Corinthians 12:28-31).

* Once God gives a gift, it will not be withdrawn or recalled (Romans 11:29).

(Also see Proverbs 18:16; 17:8.)

15

What Scriptural Evidences are Used to Teach that the Gifts have Ceased?

Not every Bible teacher today acknowledges the validity of speaking with other tongues, the gifts of the Spirit and other supernatural manifestations for the church today. Few question that they were part of the experience of the New Testament church but what some do question is that they are to function the same way today as they did then.

The following are some of the most common passages used to support these viewpoints:

* **I Corinthians 13:8-12** -- *"Charity never faileth: but whether there be prophecies, they shall fail; whether there be tongues, they shall cease; whether there be knowledge, it shall vanish away. For we know in part, and we prophesy in part. But when that which is perfect is come, then that which is in part shall be done away. What I was a child, I spake as a child, I understood as a child, I thought as a child: but when I became a man, I put away childish things. For now we see through a glass, darkly; but then face to face: now I know in part; but then shall I know even as also I am known."*

It is said by many that this proves tongues and prophecy (usually all supernatural utterance gifts) were to cease when the Scriptures were completed. This is said to be the meaning of verse 8-10. That which is *"perfect"* is assumed to be the completed canon of Scripture.

This, however, is a misunderstanding and misinterpretation of the passage. Connect the flow of thought in this passage with another by the same author, namely esians 4:11-16. We find in both passages Paul rasts that which is perfect (mature) with that which part (immature). The clear contrast is childhood versus manhood in both passages. Note also the similar emphasis on love in Ephesians 4:2, 15, 16.

Both of these passages speak of the church corporately growing into full manhood, which is a progressive, continuing and future process. Paul uses himself to illustrate this point. He said when he became a mature, full-grown man, he put away the things of childhood. Likewise, when the church grows up to full maturity and sees Christ *"face to face"* (I Corinthians 13:12), then will these gifts cease. (Compare with I John 3:2.)

Also, the idea of *"perfect"* (*teleios*, Gk) in the New Testament carries more strongly the idea of a spiritual, qualitative kind of completeness in the saints, rather than the idea of a completed book. The perfection referred to here is in reference to the people of God, not the Bible. Only when viewed this way does it become consistent with the great love theme of the chapter. Paul is talking of a time when *"we"* (I Corinthians 13:9), the church, come into perfection or maturity.

In addition, evidence from highly interpretive or controversial passaages should never be used to cancel out other clear statements of Scripture. A basic principle of hermeneutics is *"from the plain to the obscure."*

Rather than gifts being withdrawn because of maturity in the present order, gifts increase with maturity. Their withdrawal leaves the body in a state of helplessness.

* The ultra-dispensationalist attempts to relegate supernatural manifestations to the apostolic age. Many teach that supernatural manifestations of the Spirit (especially tongues, prophecy and miracles) cease after the apostles, and were not meant to continue.

Here are a few references which confirm the continuity

of the supernatural gifts and manifestations among believers:

Matthew 28:19-20 -- *"Go ye therefore, and teach all nations, baptizing them in the name of the Father, and of the Son, and of the Holy Ghost: teaching them to observe all things whatsoever I have commanded you: and, lo, I am with you alway, even unto the end of the world. Amen."*

Mark 16:15-17 -- *"And He said unto them, Go ye into all the world, and preach the gospel to every creature. He that believeth and is baptized shall be saved; but he that believeth not shall be damned. And these signs shall follow them that believe; in My name shall they cast out devils; they shall speak with new tongues..."*

John 14:12 -- *"Verily, verily, I say unto you, He that believeth on Me, the works that I do shall he do also; and greater works than these shall he do; because I go unto My Father."*

Acts 2:38-39 -- *"Then Peter said unto them, Repent, and be baptized every one of you in the name of Jesus Christ for the remission of sins, and ye shall receive the gift of the Holy Ghost." For the promise is unto you, and to your children, and to all that are afar off, even as many as the Lord our God shall call."*

The thought is also taught that only the twelve apostles exercised supernatural gifts. Notice, however, that the church at Corinth had all the gifts and especially practiced tongues (I Corinthians 1:5-7 and Chapters 12 and 14). We see Philip in Samaria seeing mighty miracles (Acts 8). Also we notice Philip had four daughters who prophesied (Acts 21:8-9).

Some also say that the twelve apostles were the only ones who spoke in tongues on the day of Pentecost. In Acts 2:1 it says *"they"* were all in one accord in one place, without specifying who *"they"* were or how many were there. The most likely antecedent to the *"they"* would be the same group referred to in Acts 1:13-14.

Also, when *"they"* spoke in tongues, it was *"noised abroad"* (Acts 2:6). Able scholars tell us that this does not just mean that the news spread by word of mouth, but that the noise was actually heard all around and attracted many thousand people. This supports the position that it was a large group speaking in tongues and not just the twelve. In addition, Acts 2:7-12, states that at least fifteen different languages or dialects were spoken. Either there were more than twelve or some of them spoke in more than one tongue.

Acts 2:15-18 -- *"For these are not drunken, as ye suppose, seeing it is but the third hour of the day. But this is that which was spoken by the prophet Joel; And it shall come to pass in the last days, saith God, I will pour out of My Spirit upon all flesh: and your sons and your daughters shall prophesy, and your young men shall see visions, and your old men shall dream dreams: And on my servants and on My handmaidens I will pour out in those days of My Spirit; and they shall prophesy."*

Notice that Peter, when explaining what *"these"* (vs.15) were doing, said that Joel's prophecy was being demonstrated, which spoke of the Spirit being poured out on all flesh. One of the most outstanding things about this prophecy was that the Spirit would be poured on the young and old, and on both men and women. We know there were more than twelve, that men and women were both involved, and that they were *"all"* filled with the Holy Ghost and spoke in tongues (Acts 2:4).

It is also argued that the ministry of the apostles was unique and had no successors. We should make it clear that (1) the twelve apostles did have a unique ministry in divine inspiration to deliver to the church in Scripture, and (2) all succeeding apostolic and prophetic ministry must not add to or change the inerrant Word, rather, build upon it. But Scripture makes it clear that the gifts and the ministry of the apostle (and prophet) were to continue throughout the church age. Ephesians 4:11-16 shows that all the five-fold ascension gift ministries of

Christ will be needed to bring the church into perfection. In addition, there are many men spoken of in the New Testament as apostles who were not of the original twelve:

Matthias -- Acts 1:26
Barnabas -- Acts 13:1-3; 14:4; Galatians 2:9;
    I Corinthians 19:5-6
Junia -- Romans 16:7
Adronicus -- Romans 16:7
Appollos -- I Corinthians 4:6-9; 3:5
James -- Galatians 1:19; James 1:1
Silas -- I Thessalonians 1:1; 2:6
Timothy -- I Thessalonians 1:1; 2:6
Titus -- II Corinthians 8:23
Epaphroditus -- Philippians 2:25
Paul -- Galatians 1:1; 2:8

This particular view goes on to teach that because only the apostles received the original baptism of the Spirit, others only receive the Spirit and supernatural gifts if the apostles laid hands on them personally; and that even then the gifts only operated in those they laid hands on and could not be passed on to any third party.

Yet Scripture shows that others besides the twelve did receive a direct (immediate) baptism of the Spirit (Acts 10:44-48). And that others received the baptism in the Spirit without having the original twelve lay hands on them (Acts 9:17; 19:6). Many other Christians did have spiritual gifts (I Corinthians 12:7; 14:12,26,31). It is the teaching of Paul that *"every"* believer should have supernatural manifestations of the Holy Spirit. Notice also that Timothy received gifts by the laying on of Paul's hands and prophecy (II Timothy 1:6; I Timothy 4:14). Also see Paul's statements concerning his call in Galatians 1:15-17.

* **I Corinthians 12:31 - 13:2** -- *"But covet earnestly the best gifts: and yet shew I unto you a more excellent way. Though I speak with the tongues of men and of angels, and have not charity, I am become as sounding brass, or a* *tinkling cymbal. And though I have the gift of prophecy, and understand all mysteries, and all knowledge; and though I have all faith, so that I could remove mountains, and have not charity, I am nothing."*

A third view says that Paul, here, divorces gifts and love; that he says if you have love that you do not need gifts, because they are for the "childhood" stage. Love, being the greatest, superceeds gifts and makes them unnecessary.

Yet 14:1 of the same book gives us Paul's real message: *"Follow after charity, and desire spiritual gifts."* It is gifts combined with love that is the *"more excellent way" (12:31).* He says that gifts without love are as sounding brass and a tinkling cymbal, but that it is not to say gifts are bad any more than we can say that money is evil simply because some misuse it. We can only express the divine nature as we have both His love and miraculous manifestations. The ideal is not one without the other, but both in proper balance.

I Corinthians 12, 13, 14 gives us a very important principle when surveyed as a unit. Chapter 12 speaks of the gifts, Chapter 13 emphasizes love, and Chapter 14 emphasizes the blending of both in practical outworking.

* **Mark 16:16-20** -- *"He that believeth and is baptized shall be saved; but he that believeth not shall be damned. And these signs shall follow them that believe; In My name shall they cast out devils; they shall speak with new tongues; they shall take up serpents; and if they drink any deadly thing, it shall not hurt them; they shall lay hands on the sick, and they shall recover. So then after the Lord had spoken unto them, He was received up into heaven, and sat on the right hand of God. And they went forth, and preached every where, the Lord working with them, and confirming the Word with signs following. Amen."*

This passage is perhaps the most difficult passage to deal with for those who would question the authenticity of the gifts of the Spirit for today. For this reason it is one of the most disputed passages in the New Testament. Many believe that this portion of Scripture was not included in the original manuscripts. Regardless of how you stand on this particular passage, the truths found in this passage are clearly confirmed by the remainder of the New Testament and early Christian history as well.

We could quote from Irenaeus of the second century down to men of modern times who wrote of spiritual gifts being manifested in every century since Christ. Even between the twelfth and fifteenth centuries, God moved mightily in parts of Europe. Among the Waldenses and Albigneses there were manifestations of the Spirit. Physical healing was a part of their written confession. Tongues were common among the Jensenists, the early Quakers, the converts of Wesley and Whitefield, and the Irvingites. The Catholic Jesuits persecuted the Jensenists because of their gifts of healing, tongues, discerning of spirits, and prophecy. And even later (1876) we find that young men spoke in tongues and prophesied under the ministry of D.L. Moody. This is documented in the book *Trials and Triumphs of Faith,* by Robert Boyd, who was an intimate friend of Moody.

The Gifts of the Holy Spirit

WORD OF WISDOM

WORD OF KNOWLEDGE

DISCERNING of SPIRITS

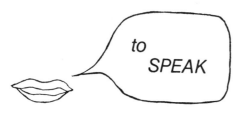

PROPHECY

TONGUES

INTERPRETATION of TONGUES

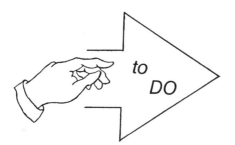

HEALING

MIRACLES

FAITH

16

Practical Instructions in the Operation of the Gifts

The Scriptures confirm that, though the gifts are the manifestation of the Holy Spirit, God operates through a person as a cooperative act; man does not become a puppet, or act unconsciously, or go into a trance. Rather, he must cooperate with the Lord to express *what* God wants to say *in the way* God wants it expressed.

There is a difference between reacting to the Holy Spirit and responding to Him. Often, in the operation of gifts, there is so much human reaction or human excess that an element of confusion is brought in and people do not receive from it what they might. We can illustrate this using electricity: when you put a bulb in an electrical socket, you have a beautiful, constructive response to electricity; if you remove the bulb and insert your finger, there will be a reaction to that same electricity.

Now, just learning to know facts and principles, as we will be doing in this book, is one way of learning to cooperate with the Spirit. Yet much of it can be learned only by a living union with the Spirit. There is growth development in this area, just as with anything else, as one becomes more sensitive to the Holy Spirit.

We should mention here that more practical instruction is usually required where the vocal gifts are concerned. Paul went into more detail on tongues, interpretation and prophecy than any of the others because they are the gifts which involve communication to the whole body. Because the gifts involve communicating to the whole body, it is very important that they operate with order and coherence. When abuses occur in this area, confusion is brought to the whole body, and Paul's goal was to edify the body, not confuse it.

The gifts of the Spirit are to be subject to the written Word of God:

I John 5:11 -- *"This is THE record..."* (emphasis added).

I Corinthians 14:37 -- *"If any man think himself to be a prophet, or spiritual, let him acknowledge that the things that I write unto you are the commandments of the Lord."*

Revelation 22:18,19 -- *"For I testify unto every man that heareth the words of the prophecy of this book, If any man shall add unto these things, God shall add unto him the plagues that are written in this book: and if any man shall take away from the words of the book of this prophecy, God shall take away his part out of the book of life, and out of the holy city, and from the things which are written in this book."*

Deuteronomy 4:2 -- *"Ye shall not add unto the word which I command you, neither shall ye diminish ought from it, that ye may keep the commandments of the Lord your God which I command you."*

Proverbs 30:5-6 -- *"Every word of God is pure: He is a shield unto them that put their trust in Him. Add thou not unto His words, lest He reprove thee, and thou be found a liar."*

Though it is true the Spirit still speaks, He will never *"add"* to this Book, in the sense of contradicting or changing its truth.

Ephesians 2:20 -- *"And are built upon the foundation of the apostles and prophets, Jesus Christ Himself being the chief corner stone."*

NOTE: Paul did not say that the apostles built the whole building, rather they laid the foundation. We simply build on what they taught; go on from where they brought us. Their doctrine is final and authoritative, and has God's seal of approval.

No matter how sure one is that he has a spiritual revelation or a word from the Lord, if it contradicts the clear teaching of the Scripture, it must not be accepted. Our only safety from error is to stay within the boundaries of revealed truth.

The gifts of the Spirit are to be subject to the oversight ministries of the local church:

The Scripture clearly teaches that God holds leaders accountable for the spiritual health and well-being of the flock. Someone must stand accountable and responsible for everything that is said or done in the church. A failure to observe this is one of the greatest errors of the many gatherings of believers where gifts operate, but without oversight present. This is, in fact, the means which the Lord has provided to see to it that all is done in accordance with the Scripture.

Ephesians 4:11-15 shows the ministry was given to bring the saints to maturity so that they would not be like a little ship in the ocean, *"tossed to and fro, and carried about with every wind of doctrine, by the sleight of men, and cunning craftiness, whereby they lie in wait to deceive; but speaking the truth in love, may grow up into Him in all things, which is the head, even Christ."*

Acts 20:28-30 -- *"Take heed therefore unto yourselves, and to all the flock over the which the Holy Ghost hath made you overseers, to feed the church of God, which He hath purchased with His own blood. For I know this, that after my departing shall grievous wolves enter in among you, not sparing the flock. Also of your own selves shall men arise speaking perverse things, to draw away disciples after them."*

Hebrews 13:17 -- *"Obey them that have the rule over you, and submit yourselves: for they watch for your souls, as they that must give account, that they may do it with joy, and not with grief: for that is unprofitable for you."*
James 3:1 -- *"My brethren, be not many masters, knowing that we shall receive the greater condemnation."*

Though God does not have one standard of life for the ministry and another for the flock, the ministry is held responsible not only for their own walk, but also the welfare of others.

Proverbs 27:23 -- *"Be thou diligent to know the state of thy flocks, and look well to thy herds."*

(Also see: I Peter 5:2; John 10:11-13; II Corinthians 7:12; Ezekiel 33:6; Jeremiah 23:4.)

II Corinthians 8:23 tells us that the ministering brethren are the *"messengers of the churches, and the glory of Christ."*

Even the prophets must be willing to be judged by others (I Corinthians 14:29). How much more should we all be willing to have our gifts evaluated and judged by spiritual shepherds. This is God's means of checks and balances. If one rejects this safety measure, it is because he is wrongly motivated.

This is one of the first things a believer should take advantage of: receiving counsel of, and working closely with the elders over him as those who are *"accountable"* for him and *"feed"* him, whose occupation is *"the perfecting of the saints, for the work of the ministry"* (Ephesians 4:11-12).

Those in authority have the responsibility to correct, rebuke and admonish the believers and establish them in truth. They are to bring forth things both *"new and old"* out of their treasury to set before the saints (Matthew 13:52). It is not a matter of lording over the flock or having dominion over their faith, but the authority is spiritual and will only benefit the believer as he submits himself to it willingly and with spiritual motives (II Corinthians 1:24). Paul tells Christians that it is *"unprofitable"* not to submit (Hebrews 13:17).

The principle of leadership over gifts and ministries is illustrated in I Chronicles 25:1-7. Here we see Asaph prophesying under the guidance of King David, and the sons of Asaph, Jeduthun and Heman, prophesying and praising and singing under the direction of their fathers.

The fact that something is spiritual does not mean that it cannot be ordered, guided and judged. God knows that human error is always potentially present and has provided for its restraint and correction.

In I Peter 5:5 the Lord, through Peter, instructs the elders to be in subjection one to another as they exercise their oversight among the flock, so that no man stands alone, without the balancing influences of others upon His ministry.

Many of the dilemmas and quandaries a person may face in learning the *"ways of the Spirit"* have been faced years before in those over him in the Lord.

The spiritual elders can give valuable instruction which may save him from error or frustration. The book of Proverbs tells us to love instruction and seek it; that one who hates it despises his own soul (Proverbs 15:32).

It should be noted that chronological age and the amount of time one has been saved make very little difference unless that person has been active in spiritual operations. Those who have been saved only a year or two, yet have yielded to the operation of the gifts, will know far more about the ways of the Spirit than a person who has been a Christian for many years yet has never moved in these areas.

The principle of "yielding" your members (Romans 6:13):

I Corinthians 14:15 -- *"I will pray with the Spirit, and I will pray with the understanding also."*

This throws much light on how the Spirit works through the believer. The believer is not to be passive, but involved with his will and body; actively participating. The participation does not take place when he is in a state of unconsciousness or in some ecstatic, euphoric stupor. Rather, the participation is intelligent and voluntary.

We must obey the prompting of the Spirit by faith and the act of our will, putting ourselves into a position in which the Holy Spirit can use us and manifest Himself through us. It is important to realize that He possesses us in order to see His tools through us. We do not use the Spirit, He uses us. There are two extreme positions which should be mentioned at this point and which must be avoided:

* That gifts operate at the believer's will, so that he is free to exercise them anytime, anyplace. Some Scriptures which are used to validate this position are:

   I Corinthians 14:15 -- *"I will pray with the Spirit, and I will pray with understanding also: I will sing with the Spirit, and I will sing with the understanding also."*
   I Corinthians 14:32 -- *"The spirits of the prophets are subject to the prophets."*

   I Timothy 4:14 -- *"Neglect not the gift that is in thee."*

   II Timothy 1:6 -- *"Stir up the gift of God..."*

   The danger of this is that it makes gifts too common, and depletes their power and effect. It encourages people to be too *"fast"* and puts them in danger of getting into the emotional or soulish realm.

Some even go so far as to say that the believer has the prerogative to choose which gift he will exercise. This is often based on wrong interpretation of I Corinthians 12:18, *"But now hath God set the members every one of them in the body, as it hath pleased Him."* The *"Him"* is said to refer to the believer, who then is set in according to his own pleasing. This is in error; the *"Him"* in this Scripture refers to God.

This school of thought appeals especially to those who are extremely aggressive by personality. If a whole church practices this, it can lead to a survival of the fittest situation, with a few extroverts dominating, but preventing the developing of a well-rounded body ministry. It is partly due to this position that gifts have often operated in the soulish realm.

* That the believer should demand a supernatural sign before operating in a gift.

The previous extreme position mentioned is the sin of haste; this next one involves the sin of delay. Both can quench and grieve the Spirit.

In the operation of a gift, an *"unction"* (I John 2:20) or a revelation and prompting of the Spirit is needed, but this does not involve expecting presumptuous signs.
I Corinthians 14:30 -- *"If any thing be revealed to another that sitteth by, let the first hold his peace."*

Even a prophet had to wait for something to be revealed before he could speak the word of the Lord.

II Peter 1:21 -- *"For the prophecy came not in old time by the will of man: but holy men of God spake as they were moved by the Holy Ghost."*

Scripture was written while holy men were being *"moved"* and borne along by the Holy Spirit.

Notice the special reference to Peter's being *"filled with the Holy Ghost"* when he spoke before the Jewish council (Acts 4:8), and also the reference to Paul in Acts 13:9-11, when the gifts of wisdom, knowledge and discerning of spirits operated through him.

So, the gifts do not function at will, rather, upon divine demand. God brings us face to face with a need or situation, then quickens us to operate to meet that need.

We should not wait for the Spirit to overwhelm us with a lot of emotional feelings. The gifts spring from our spirits, not from our emotions. The emotions may be affected, but gifts do not originate there.

When a person is just beginning to operate in the gifts, however, it has been commonly experienced by many that God seems to give greater signs and assurance. Then after a period of growth, He gradually removes a measure of them and requires more faith and sensitivity on the part of the believer. But God does not take away the consciousness or control, or violate the freedom of one's will (I Corinthians 14:32).

We must not be guilty of indulging in the Corinthians' excess: acting out of order or when not under the compulsion of the Holy Spirit, or refusing to act and by delay, preventing the Spirit from moving through us. Both can involve us in soulish extremes. One moves too fast and becomes a real mixture. The other leans too much on feelings and soulishly-sensed inspiration. The balance between the Spirit taking the initiative and the person taking the initiative is not so much stated as it is sensed. It must be learned subjectively by each individual, as well as through being subject to counsel and correction.

Gifts are to be governed by love:

This is the whole message of I Corinthians 13. It is not accident that in the design of Scripture, God permeates the subject of the gifts with the emphasis of love. The love chapter is actually an integral part of the teaching on the gifts.

Jesus taught, *"Ye shall know them by their fruits"* (Matthew 7:16), and the fruit of the Spirit is always the real test of quality of ministry (Galatians 5:22-26). If love is weak, the gifts will not have their full effect. The fruit of the Spirit and the quality of love is what gives gifts their full authority and power to minister to others. Without these, the gifts can become as *"a sounding brass and a tinkling cymbal"* (I Corinthians 13:1).

We must walk in the Spirit as well as operate spiritual gifts. If we walk in the flesh and occasionally operate a gift, it will not be charged with spiritual vitality. Rather, it will carry a note of superficiality.

I Corinthians 3:13-15 -- *"Every man's work shall be made manifest: for the day shall declare it, because it shall be revealed by fire; and the fire shall try every man's work of what sort it is. If any man's work abide which he hath built there upon, he shall receive a reward. If any man's work shall be burned, he shall suffer loss: but he himself shall be saved; yet so as by fire."*

Jonah demonstrates that a prophet can operate without love and it will profit him nothing, even though in Jonah's case, it did bless and save Ninevah. This is what Paul spells out to the Corinthians in I Corinthians 3:13-15. We may operate a gift strictly on faith, but if we lack personal quality, it will profit nothing in the hereafter. And even though others may receive some benefit from it here, they cannot receive its full potential if we lack love.

It is not enough to function simply out of faith or obedience. Our motives must go beyond that and be based on love for God's people. We can function by faith and have mixed motives. It is not the right motive to just not want to fail God, or to be anxious to see that our ministry functions. These motives can be mixed with much human ambition and concern about "my gift," rather than concern for those to whom it is to minister. The motive for *"stirring up our gift"* must not stop short of Paul's: *"For the love of*

Christ constraineth us" (II Corinthians 5:14).

Galatians 5:6 tells us that even faith is to work *"by love."* Many of the problems of the past, both in the flock and among the leaders, have been based on a violation of these principles of love.

The principle of "edification":

I Corinthians 14:12 -- *"Even so ye, forasmuch as ye are zealous of spiritual gifts, seek that ye may excel to the edifying of the church."*

I Corinthians 14:26 -- *"Let all things be done unto edifying."*

I Corinthians 8:1 -- *"Knowledge puffeth up, but charity edifieth."*

According to the thoughts in these verses, when we do things that do not edify, then it is doubtful that we are motivated by love.

II Corinthians 10:8 -- *"For though I should boast somewhat more of our authority, which the Lord hath given us for edification, and not for your destruction."*

II Corinthians 12:19 -- *"We speak before God in Christ: but we do all things, dearly beloved, for your edifying."*

(See also Romans 15:2; Ephesians 4:12,29; I Thessalonians 5:11; I Timothy 1:4; I Corinthians 14:5.)

The whole premise upon which the 14th Chapter of I Corinthians was written was that it is possible to operate a gift in a manner which does not edify the church. Notice that the consideration is not just that the person operating the gift be edified or even a part of the body, but the whole church. Every action and operation should be weighed by this: *"Does it edify?"* *"How will it affect the church?"* and

"How can this gift operate for the greatest benefit of the body?"

I Corinthians 14:33 shows us that God is not the source of that which brings confusion and disturbance. God brings peace.

I Corinthians 14:40 shows that the pure operations of the Spirit are decent and orderly. It is not enough just to prophesy or speak in tongues; it must be done in a proper and orderly way.

This has several aspects. Some particular areas to which this applies are:

* **The manner in which it is done** -- Scripturally, no one should be abusive or an exhibitionist, or emotionally extravagant, saying that he could not control himself, that *"it was the Holy Spirit"* (I Corinthians 14:32).

We should always be open to the sovereignty of God and the unusual manifestation, but we are here referring to mainstream practice. God always reserves to Himself a two percent margin for exceptions. Yet there is a difference between God's strange sovereign acts and the strange habits of man. Which of these is being manifested can always be determined by the results which are produced.

NOTE: If one distracts by screaming a prophecy, or shaking and jerking or other physical extremes, or injects denunciations and strong negative words, the prophecy will not edify the body.

Finally, the personality of the Holy Spirit must accompany His operations (Galatians 5:22-23). If one speaks so fast that he becomes unintelligible, or is slow and repetitive, it will tend to blur the message and confuse the people. Those guilty of these faults simply need to be counselled to improve in these areas so that they may communicate more effectively. These excesses do not indicate that the gift is not of the Holy Spirit, but, rather, that the person needs to learn to yield a purer expression of the gift. The principle of spiritual manners and etiquette applies clearly to one's attitude and behavior in the gifts.

* **Timing** -- Paul tells the Corinthians not only to do things properly, but at the proper time.

In I Corinthians 14:27 he shows that tongues and interpretations should flow together with correct timing kept in mind.

In I Corinthians 14:29-33 he shows that the prophets are to flow together in their timing.

In I Corinthians 14:26 it is obvious that, in order to fulfill these practices in an orderly manner, timing is involved.

Romans 12:10 -- *"Be kindly affectioned one to another with brotherly love; in honour preferring one another."*

In other words, we should not be hoggish and dominate the meetings. This is the same principle Paul advocates in communion, which is the expressed pinnacle of our relationship (I Corinthians 11:33 -- *"tarry one for another"*). This means not being only concerned about one's own gift, but considerate of the whole body. It is generally not healthy or proper if one or two people always monopolize certain gifts just because they have the faith and freedom. They should be willing to leave room for others to be used. As long as God is able to minister, it really does not matter who He uses.

It is wrong to interrupt another in order to operate our own gift. Meetings should be conducted so that time is allowed for the function of gifts. Nor hold off or hesitate too long if the meeting is ripe and time is being allowed for the gifts to function. For example, the best time for prophecy is generally after a strong tide of worship when the *"voice of the bride"* has ascended and the *"voice of the Bridegroom"* responds (Jeremiah 33:11). It would not be nearly as edifying to wait and do it during the offering.

* The principle of unity -- It is outstanding and beautiful how the Lord builds a design in the services of the church. He usually follows a theme or a message, and everyone who is walking in the Spirit will speak the same. Even though there are *"diversities"* in gifts, *"differences"* in administration and *"diversities"* of operations, it is the same Spirit that "worketh all in all" (I Corinthians 12:4-6). As long as it is the same Spirit working through all, then there will be a unity of message and theme.

The whole idea of the church being a body speaks of a harmonious function of every organ. We should harmonize with the theme or vein of the Spirit, especially regarding the vocal gifts during a meeting, which involves God's communication system. God communicates with coherence and design. There will be some latitude, of course, within a general theme; this is illustrated by the Bible itself.

Crosscurrents should be avoided. This means being out of the mood or the message of the meeting. A cross-current is any opposing tendency or trend. It is going against the grain, or trying to check or counter something that has already been said. God brings His balances by building on what has been said; man often does it by competing with what has been said.

We may have a heavy burden or strong inner message, but if it does not fit in with what God is saying, then it is probably not to be spoken, at least at that particular time. We should not normally introduce a totally different subject or emphasis into a service. People are built up and ministered to most effectively when there is a unified theme and clarity of message.

Feeling that we could prophesy or operate a vocal gift does not always mean we should. Daniel received a vision which encompassed the entire future history of the world, but he said he *"kept the matter in my heart"* (Daniel 7:28).

Just because a message is exploding inside of our being,

does not necessarily mean it is the right delivery time. Rushing ahead actually limits the ability to be led by the Holy Spirit into greater revelation and what He wants you to do with it and when.

Even though it is God who gives a person a message, that person is still responsible to handle it properly.

Amos 3:8 -- *"The lion hath roared, who will not fear? the Lord God hath spoken, who can but prophesy?"*

The analogy is that there is as much clarity in the prophetic word as there is in the roaring of a lion.

Jeremiah 20:9 -- *"But His word was in mine heart as a burning fire shut up in my bones, and I was weary with forebearing, and I could not stay."*

Anyone can make mistakes; that is part of development. God has provided for this and knows they will occur. But we only grow with movement; while *"pressing toward the mark"* (Philippians 3:14). We learn the way of the Lord through active service, not study alone.

We must therefore begin to function according to our faith, and according to the level we are on. There is no other way to grow. We should not fear mistakes or demand an already matured ministry before we begin. This is mainly pride and fear of embarrassment.

All of us learn the way of God partly by contrast: by learning what His ways are not, as well as what they are. We must remember that as long as we remain open and teachable and submit to oversight, we will not go far astray. Those in oversight are responsible to keep the order.

To possess a gift and operate it does not mean that we are infallible. The fact that a prophetic utterance may include *"thus saith the Lord"* does not mean the Lord sanctions everything that is said or the spirit in which it is said. What is by the Holy Spirit is always true, but there remains the potential of man's thoughts and emotions being expressed. No one is exempt from this possibility. That is why the Word of God must be the final authority. The genuineness of any gift must be confirmed by the written Word and the witness of the Spirit. Therefore, no one is justified or excused when he accepts error if he does not check it with the Word and then walk in the light of the Word.

That gifts can be abused and misused is clearly demonstrated in Scripture. (See Ecclesiastes 2:9; Numbers 20:7-13 with Deuteronomy 32:48-52; I Corinthians 13:1; 14:23, 33.)

This abuse and misuse has undoubtedly caused reproach and opposition to the gifts of the Spirit. Let us take full advantage of God's safety measures that we may edify in all things.

17

What is the Gift of the Word of Wisdom?

Before we deal with each of the gifts separately, we should notice a few things by way of overall understanding and survey. When God pours out His Spirit on people, the gifts are the ways in which the Spirit manifests His presence. Therefore, as we seek for God's presence in our midst, we should not be surprised when He comes to us in these forms. To understand them gives us a concrete idea of what we are seeking and expecting from God.

These gifts fall into three groups:

Revelation gifts --

Word of wisdom
Word of knowledge
Discerning of spirits

Utterance or vocal gifts --

Tongues
Interpretation of tongues
Prophecy

Power gifts --

Faith
Healings
Miracles

The word of wisdom defined:

Remember, these are said to be manifestations of the Spirit (I Corinthians 12:7), not man's soul powers. Therefore, to just define wisdom does not adequately define this gift.

This gift cannot be gained through study and experience, yet neither is it a substitute for study and experience.

The gift of the word of wisdom is supernaturally given by God. It is not *"a"* word of wisdom but *"the"* word of wisdom. It is not just a word on the subject or the situation at hand, it is *"the word"* on it. It is the answer, the solution, or the will of God in that situation.

Natural wisdom and general wisdom are good and must be sought by all (James 1:5), yet the word of wisdom comes by means of Spirit impartation. It is not just a God-endowed faculty of human wisdom.

The word of wisdom illustrated in the life of Jesus:

We should first see this gift as it operated in the life of the Lord Jesus Himself. Jesus astonished people by: His wisdom and, His mighty works (Matthew 13:54).

Here are references which illustrate His use of the word of wisdom:

Luke 4:3-14 -- In withstanding Satan. Satan used knowledge to trap Him, but Christ went a step beyond and used divine wisdom which applied specifically to that knowledge.

Luke 7:22 -- *"Then Jesus answering said unto them, Go your way, and tell John what things ye have seen and heard; how that the blind see, the lame walk, the lepers are cleansed, the deaf hear, the dead are raised, to the poor the gospel is preached."*

His reply to John's messengers was the most masterful thing He could have said. He gave no great doctrinal explanation. He said only that they should observe His ministry and see if it bore the marks of the Son of God.

John 4:9-26 -- His ministry to the Samaritan woman. He did not side with either the Samaritans or the Judeans in their doctrines, for this would have aroused antagonism and prejudice. Rather, He led her into a greater truth and then revealed His true identity to her.

Matthew 22:21-22 -- *"Then saith He unto them, Render therefore unto Caesar the things which are Caesar's; and unto God the things that are God's. When they had heard these words, they marvelled, and left Him, and went their way."*

His answers to the Pharisees. The Pharisees threw a trick question at Him to trap Him into an offense that might open Him to accusation and legal punishment. He knew He would offend the people if He openly endorsed paying taxes, but if He opposed it, He would offend the Roman government. His answer was a word of wisdom.

How the word of wisdom is manifested:

This gift of the Spirit works in many forms for different purposes. God is a God of great variety. We tend toward attempting to stereotype Him. He has told us there are varieties of gifts and they operate in varieties of ways (I Corinthians 12:4-6).

The word of wisdom may come in the following ways:

* **By the Spirit speaking within** -- or we could say, by the spiritual intuition: hearing with the spiritual ears the voice of the Spirit.

   The book of Acts shows us repeatedly that God can and does speak without an audible voice. He imparts His mind directly through the agency of the Spirit. One just suddenly knows the mind of God on a matter. It is unexplainable except that it comes by a spiritual communication. With it also comes an instinctive faith and assurance that it is a divine *"word of wisdom."*

Acts 16:6-8 -- Here the Holy Spirit forbade Paul to go into Bythinia.

Acts 20:22-24 -- God had imparted to Paul the *"word of wisdom"* and he knew he was to press toward Jerusalem even though he had received the prophetic word that bonds and afflictions awaited. Some have criticized Paul for going in spite of warnings. We must remember, however, that there is a vast difference between having knowledge (even if one is a prophet) and having knowledge with wisdom. Paul knew bonds awaited him, but he also knew that this was the will of God. Notice after Agabas and Caesarean brethren could not dissuade him from going, they just committed him to the *"will"* of God (Acts 21:8-14). This was what Paul was governed by all along. He went to Rome as *"prisoner of the Lord,"* not of Rome--he said so five times (Ephesians 3:1; 4:1; II Timothy 1:8; Philemon 1,9). Notice also that right at the beginning of his imprisonment in Jerusalem, an angel confirmed that it was a part of God's plan (Acts 23:11) to get him to Rome.

Paul was eventually sent to Rome by his own choice. He intentionally appealed to Caesar to judge his case (Acts 26:32). This was to later require yet another miracle, that of preserving the ship in the storm (Acts 27).

In all of this we can see the fulfilling of God's word over Paul, spoken at his conversion: *"The Lord said unto him, Go thy way: for he is a chosen vessel unto Me, to bear My name before the Gentiles, and kings, and the children of Israel: for I will show him how great things he must suffer for My name's sake"* (Acts 9:15-16).

This inner impartation of wisdom also operates in dealing

with people's personal problems and complex situations:

I Kings 3:16-28 -- Solomon's dealings with the two harlots is a perfect example of this. This was a direct fulfillment of what the Lord had promised Solomon. The request Solomon made was that he might have discernment and wisdom to judge the people (I Kings 3:9).

II Samuel 12:1-14 -- Here we see that the prophet Nathan not only had supernatural knowledge, but supernatural wisdom and guidance in the application of that knowledge.

Acts 8:20-23 -- Peter saw Simon's heart as an open book, and by the words of knowledge and wisdom, dealt with him.

Acts 23:6-10 -- Here Paul did something similar to what Christ had done in dealing with the Pharisees and Sadducees: he was given wisdom from the Lord to side with the Pharisees and thus cause dissension among the people.

It takes God to discern the thoughts and motives of men's hearts (Hebrews 4:12).

The word of wisdom often is given to leaders in counselling others. It may even operate without the person being used, knowing it.

People can often hide their real problems effectively and present to a leader only what they want him to hear. Or they may be confused as to what the real answer to their problem is, and it often requires a Spirit-imparted word of wisdom to bring clarity and direction.

When the Spirit gives a word of wisdom, a crisis is then created, breaking down the opposition, and we either yield to God's word or openly rebel against it.

* **As a revealed application of Scripture** -- this would be a *"quickened word from the Lord"* for a specific situation

(Psalm 119:50, 154). It brings a real live need in touch with the voice of God through the Scripture.

Acts 1:15-23 -- As Peter and the rest of the 120 were in prayer, God opened to his understanding what should be done. He did it by quickening a Scripture to Peter. He used Psalm 69:25 and 109:8, where David was praying a prayer against his enemies.

Acts 2:14-36 -- The word of wisdom was also involved here in the revealing of Old Testament Scripture to Peter.

Acts 15:13-18 -- Here James is given the word of wisdom and revelation concerning an Old Testament passage helping bring the solution to a very thorny problem in the early church.

* By an audible voice or an angel --

I Kings 19:12-18 -- God speaks in the still small voice to Elijah, telling him what he is to do.

Acts 8:26, 29 -- In verse 26, the angel of the Lord spoke to Philip, then verse 29 specifies that it was the Spirit speaking to him.

Acts 9:10-16 -- We see that an audible voice came to Ananias, instructing him concerning what he was to do.

Acts 27:23-24 -- The angel appeared to Paul and revealed God's word concerning the situation.

* By dreams, visions and trances --

Acts 18:9-10 -- The Lord spoke to Paul in a night vision assuring him that no harm would come to him, and that there were many godly people in Corinth.

Acts 16:9-10 -- The Macedonian call came to Paul in a vision at night.

Acts 22:17-21 -- Jesus Himself appeared to Paul,

instructing him as to what he was to do.

Acts 10:1-6 -- It was through a vision that the Lord spoke to Cornelius, showing him what to do.

Acts 10:10-17 -- Peter went into a trance and was instructed by God. The word *"trance"* is defined by Vincent's Expository Dictionary as, *"a condition in which ordinary consciousness and the perception of natural circumstances were withheld, and the soul was susceptible only to the vision imparted by God."* This was not a self-induced trance, but Spirit induced. It was a temporary oblivion to the natural realm, just as the prophets often experienced when being shown fantastic spiritual realities.

* By the unanimity of the Spirit among spiritual leaders--

Acts 6:1-6 -- When they were confronted with a major problem requiring a major decision, God gave a word of wisdom to the twelve which set the direction, not only for their situation, but for the church down through history. Deacons became a permanent office and function in the local church. This is later confirmed by Paul in I Timothy 3:8-13.

Acts 15:2, 4, 6, 22, 23 -- It was through the plurality of ministry that a great crisis was met. It was solved by the apostolic vision of Peter; the apostolic results of the ministry of Paul and Barnabas; the quickening of a word of wisdom and revelation from the Old Testament to the apostle James; and the unity of the Spirit among all the apostles and elders.

* In connection with prophecy concerning future events and developments -- this may include the unfolding of God's plans for the future concerning nations, places, cities, or even individuals. The word of wisdom is expressed not so much in the foretelling of events as in those commands and instructions which God gives arising out of His knowledge of those events. In such cases it is only as certain events develop over a period of time that the word of wisdom is fulfilled.

II Kings 8:1-6 -- There was a warning of a seven year famine and instructions to the widow and her family to leave the country.

Daniel 5:17-29 -- God knew the armies were diverting the channel of the river in order to gain entrance into the city under the great impregnable wall which protected it, and Daniel, by a prophetic word and word of wisdom, explained God's purpose through it all.

Acts 18:10-11 -- Paul saw by divine wisdom and knowledge the great Corinthian church when it had not yet been formed: *"For I have much people in this city."*

Other observations and principles:

The word of wisdom operates with, and may include, any of the other gifts as the occasion may demand.

Acts 9:34 -- Peter operated in wisdom and healing and knowledge (probably miracles and faith also).

Acts 18:8-12 -- Paul, when in a complicated situation, was given a word of wisdom as to how to handle it. It was accompanied by a word of knowledge, faith, miracles and prophecy.

Acts 14:9-10 -- Paul was given wisdom, or divine perception, into what God wanted done in this man's life. It was accompanied by at least the gifts of faith, miracles, and knowledge.

Acts 16:16-18 -- Again, after a period of time, the Lord directed Paul with an impartation of divine wisdom for this occasion. It was also accompanied by faith, knowledge and the discerning of spirits.

Acts 16:25-32 -- Paul and Silas did not instinctively make a break for freedom, rather, God directed them with a timely word of wisdom to lead this jailer and his family to the Lord.

(For other related Scriptures see: Daniel 2:30; II Samuel 5:19, 23-24; Proverbs 11:30; Acts 6:3,10; I Kings 10:1; Genesis 41:33-36).

NOTE: I Corinthians 1:17-31 differentiates between worldly wisdom and God's wisdom. (Also see James 3:14-18.)

The power and the place of the word of wisdom:

It is the first gift mentioned and is needed in the operation of all of the other gifts.

Ephesians 1:17 -- *"That the God of our Lord Jesus Christ, the Father of glory, may give unto you the spirit of wisdom and revelation in the knowledge of Him."*

Wisdom is connected with a deep intimate knowledge of God.

Colossians 1:9 -- *"For this cause we also, since the day we heard it, do not cease to pray for you, and to desire that ye might be filled with the knowledge of His will in all wisdom and spiritual understanding."*

II Peter 3:15 -- *"And account that the longsuffering of our Lord is salvation; even as our beloved brother Paul also according to the wisdom given unto him hath written unto you."*

Proverbs 8:22-30 -- Gives Christ His rightful place with regard to the subject of divine wisdom. He is the wisdom of God personified and embodied. (Also I Corinthians 1:24.)

Wisdom itself is the ability to apply possessed knowledge and experience. It involves dealing with affairs on a practical, working level as distinguished from mere study and investigation. Knowledge is the raw material; wisdom is needed to build with it.

NOTE: In Proverbs 2:10 and I Kings 10:24, wisdom is connected with the heart.

We need spiritual wisdom in governing the affairs of our daily lives and in the winning of souls, as well as for personal guidance, etc. The day may come when we will be called before *"magistrates"* and civil powers. Jesus promised us *"words of wisdom"* in such cases (Matthew 18:19). There is great power and strength in godly wisdom and understanding.

Proverbs 24:3-6 -- *"Through wisdom is an house builded; and by understanding it is established: and by knowledge shall the chambers be filled with all precious and pleasant riches. A wise man is strong; yea, a man of knowledge increaseth strength. For by wise counsel thou shalt make thy war: and in multitude of counsellors there is safety."*

Proverbs 3:19 -- *"The Lord by wisdom hath founded the earth; by understanding hath He established the heavens."*

Proverbs 8:14 -- *"Counsel is mine, and sound wisdom: I am understanding; I have strength."*

James 1:5 -- *"If any of you lack wisdom, let him ask of God, that giveth to all men liberally, and upbraideth not; and it shall be given him."*

The gift of wisdom will play a tremendous part in the last day church. It is vital that we have the *"mind of Christ"* on all issues of the Kingdom of God.

18

What is the Gift of The Word of Knowledge?

Notice the prominence given to wisdom and knowledge. This is in keeping with the general tenor of Scripture. It is especially the order of things in the book of Proverbs.

Chapter One and verse two of Proverbs tells that the Proverbs were written to give wisdom (God's wisdom), and in verse seven, we are told that the fear of the Lord is the beginning of knowledge.

Wisdom, knowledge and understanding are constant and recurring themes in the Bible. Notice how these two New Testament verses combine them: *"O the depth of the riches both of the wisdom and knowledge of God"* (Romans 11:33); *"In Whom are hid all the treasure of wisdom and knowledge"* (Colossians 2:3).

So God places a premium on these, not only in the general functions of man and his relationships to life, but in relation to God Himself and Christ and the work of redemption, as well as relating to the manifestations of the Holy Spirit through man in spiritual gifts.

Proverbs 24:3-5 shows us that it is by wisdom and knowledge that we build that which is permanent. Many of the needs in the local church and the lives of believers do not require material miracles or a great miraculous deliverance, rather the impartation of wisdom and knowledge and understanding. This is what brings great spiritual release and joy and power in our lives.

All the other gifts and operations of the Spirit build on these and are to be governed and guided by them. It is a real error to try to build something permanent on any basis other than wisdom and knowledge. Therefore, these should be strongly emphasized and sought, especially by those in leadership, as being among the *"best gifts"* (I Corinthians 12:31).

Jesus gave a provocative principle in Luke 7:35 when He said, *"Wisdom is justified of all her children."* In other words, wisdom is proven by what it produces.

Wisdom and knowledge produce good fruit. The real test of any work or ministry lies in that which it produces over a period of time.

The word of knowledge defined:

The word of knowledge is the supernatural revelation to man of some detail of the knowledge of God. It is the impartation of facts and information which are humanly impossible to know. It is not knowledge that comes through natural ability, observation, study, education or experience. It is knowledge that surpasses the senses of man. It goes beyond knowledge that is obtainable by any natural means. This is the nature of all the gifts of the Spirit. They are not expressions of man's ability, but are said to be the *"manifestations of the Spirit"* (I Corinthians 12:7).

I Corinthians 13:9-10 -- *"For we know in part, and we prophesy in part. But when that which is perfect is come, then that which is in part shall be done away."*

The word of knowledge is a portion of God's knowledge.

What kind of knowledge does this involve?

And, it may be added, for what purpose is it revealed?

It may be knowledge of the thought of men's hearts -- Luke

5:22; 6:8; 7:36-50; 13:11-13; Matthew 3:7-12. It may involve men's plans such as Ahab in I Kings 21:17-20; or motives, as in Luke 6:8.

It may be knowledge of facts of the past, present or future. John 1:1-5 is a revelation of the pre-incarnate Christ; in John 11:11-14 Christ saw that Lazarus had already died; in Acts 11:27-30 the prophet Agabus saw the coming famine.

It may reveal the whereabouts of men -- I Samuel 10:1-24; Acts 9:10-18; 10:5-6; 16:9-10.

Or warning of coming danger -- II Kings 6:9; Acts 20:28-30.

It may expose hypocrisy -- II Kings 5:20-27; Matthew 23:13-39; Mark 12:13-17; Luke 12:1-12.

It may reveal deception -- I Kings 14:2-6; Acts 5:1-10.

God reveals such things as are necessary for the furtherance of His will and purposes among any given people. He will normally reveal these things to key people or those who are in positions of responsibility or loving concern over others. He does it, not just to inform, but to bring the necessary changes and adjustments required. Often, there is a relationship to a physical need, and God reveals this to one who has the necessary faith and gifts of healing to deliver the sick person.

Scriptural examples of the word of knowledge:

In the life of Christ:

John 11:11-14 -- concerning the death of Lazarus.

John 4:17-18 -- exposing the life of the Samaritan woman.

John 13:38 -- concerning Peter's denial of Him.

John 6:61 -- concerning the murmuring of the disciples at

His teaching.

(See also Luke 6:8; 5:22; 7:36-50; 13:16.)

In the life of Joseph:

Genesis 40:5-19 -- concerning the dreams of the butler and the baker.

Genesis 41:1-36 -- concerning Pharoah's dream and the seven-year famine. (Notice the word of wisdom and the word of knowledge operating together.)

In Samuel's life:

I Samuel 3:11-14 -- concerning the impending judgment on the priesthood of Eli and his sons.

I Samuel 8:6-18 -- concerning the manner of the coming king.

I Samuel 13:14 -- concerning the removal of Saul's dynasty.

In Elisha's life:

II Kings 8:7-12 -- concerning the death of Ben-Hadad and the coming reign of Hazael.

In Daniel's life:

Daniel 2:19-45 -- concerning Nebuchadnezzar's dream. (Again note the word of wisdom and supernatural knowledge intertwined.)

Daniel 5 -- concerning Belshazzar's judgment.

In the life of Peter:

Matthew 16:16 -- Peter knew Jesus was the Christ by

divine knowledge.

Acts 5:1-11 -- concerning the deceit of Ananias and Sapphira.

In the life of Paul:

Acts 20:29-31 -- concerning false prophets in the Ephesian church.

Acts 27:10-24 -- concerning the safety of their journey.

Acts 18:9-10 -- concerning Corinth and his ministry there.

How is the word of knowledge manifested?

The word of knowledge, just as the word of wisdom, may be manifested in a variety of ways (I Corinthians 12:6).

It may come in a vision or a dream -- Hosea 12:10; Amos 1:1; Obadiah 1:1; Acts 10:9-20.

It may come by a definite impression of the Holy Spirit, or the inner voice of the Spirit. See the principle used in Romans 8:16; John 14:26; and, 16:13-14.

It may come by an audible voice -- Ezekiel 43:6; Acts 10:13-20.

Or it can come as an angel -- Acts 27:22-26; 8:26; 10:1-6.

It may come by the quickening of the Scriptures -- Psalm 119:18; Acts 1:15-23; 15:13-21. Notice that the word of wisdom and the word of knowledge are operating together.

Also, many have experienced a deposit of a word of knowledge as they talked or counselled or wrote letters, or even while praying for someone.

Instructions in operating the word of knowledge:

Remember, the fact that something is revealed does not necessarily mean it should be spoken immediately, or even spoken at all. A word of knowledge often comes unexpectedly, and is often for the purpose of bringing us to prayer concerning what God shows us. It may involve a need in someone's life or family, or in a local church or city. The purpose of God in revealing the knowledge is to give the right people the necessary knowledge and instruction to see His people fully walk in His ways.

This, of course, is a general statement and applies to many levels of knowledge.

We must remember, too, that the word of knowledge is not essentially a vocal gift. It may be received by silent revelation and the recipient should ask God to show him what to do with it. If it is a dream or vision, we should seek God for a sure interpretation (just as one who speaks in tongues should pray to interpret -- I Corinthians 14:13). Such knowledge should not be made public or shared as a sure word from God until it is clear and strong and unmistakably from the Lord. If we tell people that God told us something which does not prove out, we will lose much authority and our leadings from God will be questioned.

One of the cardinal mistakes is to announce publicly and abroad things which God wants shared only with the people involved. This may be done because of an ambitious spirit or a desire to appear superspiritual, both are sins. We can edify and bring deliverance if we use this gift wisely, or we can embarrass and bring ruin if we become too indulgent. Since this gift will often relate to the personal lives of individuals, privacy and confidentiality should be observed when appropriate.

When we have what we believe to be a word of knowledge, which relates to important issues, and we are not sure how to handle it, then it should be shared with the pastor or elders (or both) so that God might give wisdom and direction.

To maintain the flow of the gifts at their top capacity and maximum effect we must not use them to draw excessive attention to ourselves. Our own words should be few and humble, not playing it up big. We should commune much with God and give ourselves to prayer and the Word, and build ourselves up by praying in the Spirit. One of the best antidotes for pride is to stay broken before God in our devotional life.

There may be times when a word of knowledge will come in a meeting through prophecy. This may be a warning or caution to someone whom God knows is living in sin or is about to make a major mistake. When given in this general setting, no one may know who is being spoken to except the one being warned. This may also happen to give direction or specific guidance to someone present.

Though the word of knowledge is not primarily for interpreting the Scripture, it does work in that area at times. Notice in I Corinthians 13:2, Paul appears to connect the gift of knowledge and prophecy with understanding divine mysteries. Paul spoke about the special revelation and knowledge he had of the mysteries of God in several places (Ephesians 1:9; 3:3-4). This was given to him as divinely imparted knowledge. The enlightenment of the Scriptures in our day and time involves the gift of knowledge to a degree.

We are admonished to *"covet earnestly the best gifts."* But what are the best gifts? The best gift is that gift which will meet the immediate need most effectively. When supernatural knowledge is needed, the gift of healing would not be the *"best gift"* for that occasion.

It is beautiful to know that God is aware of every person, place and thing in existence, and is conscience of them all at the same time. Everyone on earth could pray at the same time, making varied supplication, and God would hear each prayer as though it were the only one being offered. The prayer could come from a jet plane crashing the sound barrier at a terrific rate of speed or from a submarine with jammed controls lying helpless on the floor of the ocean, God still hears and responds.

We need not fear the future, or the tribulation, or all the big questions of church pattern and order, etc. As we *"walk in the light, as He is in the light,"* we will have the necessary knowledge and illumination, and be led by God step by step as He imparts His knowledge to us. No one person or church will receive it all, but as we walk in the combined revelation of God to the church, we will find balance and safety.

19

What is "The Discerning of Spirits"?

Does the Bible reveal any information about the spirit world?

* **The Bible confirms the fact of the spiritual world** -- that there are actual incorporeal (without physical bodies) beings. In fact, these exist in great numbers and in three major realms, and have particular personalities and characters.

The Bible mentions the words *"spirit"* or *"spirits"* 990 times. Actually, all life is spirit. God breathed the spirit of life into man and he became a living soul. When the spirit leaves, the man is dead (Genesis 2:7; Ecclesiastes 8:8; 12:7; 3:18-21; James 2:26; Job 32:8; 33:4).

Even though we tend to be unconscious of the spirit world surrounding us, we are really highly influenced and controlled by it. Sinners are said to be taken captive by the devil and are controlled by his will in the spirit realm (II Timothy 2:26). This is not something weird or unusual, rather it is the way things have been since shortly after Adam was created.

It usually requires experience or contact with the spirit realm before a person is really awakened to its reality. Until then it is more a theory than reality.

* **The Bible teaches that God is a spirit and His entire realm is a spirit realm** -- Jesus teaches in John 4:24 that God is a spirit, and later the writer to the Hebrews informs us that He is also the *"Father of the spirits"* (Hebrews 12:9).

God is surrounded by spirit beings in the heavenlies. We read about angels, seraphim and cherubim, all of which are spiritual beings (Hebrews 1:7, 14; Genesis 3:24; Isaiah 6:2-6). We are also told that there are incalculable numbers of them (Daniel 7:10; Matthew 26:43). God is called the *"Lord of hosts."*

These heavenly hosts are organized into principalities and thrones. Some are higher in beauty and authority (I Peter 3:22; Colossians 1:16; Ephesians 3:10).

* **The Scripture teaches that the realm of Satan is a spirit realm** -- Satan was originally a high-ranking angel of God who fell as a result of pride, ambition and rebellion (Isaiah 14:12-15; Ezekiel 28:12-18). He has modeled his kingdom after God's, in that it has organization and system, principalities and powers (Daniel 10:12-13; John 14:30; Ephesians 2:12; 6:12). His demons are also spirits (Luke 10:17-20; I Timothy 4:1; Revelation 16:14; Matthew 12:43-45).

* **The Scripture tells us that man also has a spirit** --

I Thessalonians 5:23 -- *"And the very God of peace sanctify you wholly; and I pray God your whole spirit and soul and body be preserved blameless unto the coming of our Lord Jesus Christ."*

(Also see I Corinthians 2:11; Job 32:8; Zechariah 12:1; James 2:26.)

Just looking at these facts of the spirit world and their inter-relatedness shows us that it is impossible for us to remain neutral and unaffected by spiritual influences. The fact that we exist means we will of necessity be involved in the spirit realm and faced with dealing with spirit realities and influences.

In fact, in the present order of things, all three of these realms are at war with each other. In other words, there is a sense in which man is at war with both God's Spirit and

Satan's spirits. God is at war with the evil of man's spirit and the evil spirits of Satan. Satan and his spirits are at war with man's spirit and the Spirit of God. It is greater than a world war; it is a universal war. This is, in fact, the real battleground of good and evil; right against wrong.

Ephesians 6:11-12 -- *"Put on the whole armour of God, that ye may be able to stand against the wiles of the devil. For we wrestle not against flesh and blood, but against principalities, against powers, against the rulers of the darkness of this world, against spiritual wickedness in high places."*

This being true, God provides for the believer spiritual armor and equipment that he might have victory in this warfare (II Corinthians 10:3-5). This reference shows us that the battle is in the realm of the thoughts and the mind. It is well to remember that all thoughts are sourced in spirits. Bodies do not think; trees or inanimate objects do not think; but spirits think (I Corinthians 2:11-12). All thoughts come from one of the spirit realms. We must recognize this and resist and cast down those which come from our spirits or evil spirits, which are unclean or sinful.

What is the gift of discerning of spirits?

The gift of discerning of spirits is the God-given ability or enablement to recognize the identity (and very often the personality and condition) of the spirits which are behind different manifestations or activities.

To discern means to perceive, distinguish or differentiate. The dividing line between a human and divine operation may be obscure to some believers, but one with the faculty of spiritual discernment sees a clear separation.

Just the fact of the potential for all three of the spirit realms to be manifest through man makes this gift essential in the church.

The gift is generally imparted to shepherds of God's flock and those in positions of guarding and guiding the saints (Acts 20:29-30; Ezekiel 33:7; Mark 3:26-27).

It seems that this gift almost becomes a permanent faculty in an individual's life, operating constantly whenever any occasion for its use presents itself. And it may work on various levels. For example, one person may operate more in the realm of discerning human spirits, attitudes and needs in the lives of the saints. Another may have discernment in the areas of demonic activity. Others may be able to clearly tell which gifts and manifestations are from God and which are not, yet have little discernment in the other areas mentioned.

This gift is accompanied by a God-given ability to challenge or cope with the spirits.

What is the purpose of discerning of spirits?

Its purpose is to protect, guard, guide and properly feed the flock of God.

I John 4:1 -- *"Beloved, believe not every spirit, but try the spirits whether they are of God: because many false prophets are gone out into the world."*

Since all spirits must find expression in the material realm through the bodies and faculties of human beings, it is vital that the servants of God who face spiritual battle know and discern which spirits are being expressed.
I John 4:2-3 -- *"Hereby know ye the Spirit of God: Every spirit that confesseth that Jesus Christ is come in the flesh is of God: and every spirit that confesseth not that Jesus Christ is come in the flesh is not of God: and this is that spirit of antichrist, whereof ye have heard that it should come; and even now already is it in the world."*

By this gift we have discernment into the spirit realm. We can discern when God is moving, when it is the spirit of man operating, and when evil spirits are present and active.

NOTE: God is omnipresent (Psalm 139:7-12; 32:8; Matthew 28:20; Jeremiah 23:24) and His Spirit is constantly with and in every believer while Satan and his spirits are not omnipresent. God's Spirit is always present; evil spirits may be either present or not present. Scripture says, *"resist the devil and he will flee from you"* (James 4:7), because *"greater is He that is in you, than he that is in the world"* (I John 4:4).

This gift brings clarity, removes confusion and gives clear direction. It may remove confusion concerning the real problem we may be facing, so that we can be delivered, instructed or counselled. It may discern evil spirits and their names so that they may be cast out (Mark 9:25; 5:2-20; Luke 4:33-35; 13:11-13; Acts 16:16).

With this discernment of spirits, just as with wisdom and knowledge, comes faith to act or pray with authority. This is true of all the revelation gifts.

Satan has been known to appear as an *"angel of light"* (II Corinthians 11:13-15), and deceive even believers, but the gift of the discerning of spirits is God's provision to bring the needed protection.

It is true that some shameful things have been said and done by people claiming guidance from God. But God's Spirit and the Word of God are always in perfect agreement. So it is wise to check everything with the Word of God to see whether it is actually a revelation from God and whether it is really a duty ordered by God.

All manifestations of life are the showing forth or product of some sort of spirit. Not all manifestations, even in the local church, are of the Holy Spirit. The purpose of this gift is to bring protection, and to screen out wrong spirits from being expressed and influencing believers.

Discerning of spirits illustrated:

* In the life of Christ:

Matthew 9:4 -- *"And Jesus knowing their thoughts said, Wherefore think ye evil in your hearts?"*

Jesus knew the thoughts of the Jewish scribes which involved the spirits of men (I Corinthians 2:11). He discerned the spirits of the scribes and Pharisees many times (Matthew 12:25; Luke 5:22; 6:8; 11:17; 24:38).

Matthew 16:23 -- *"But He turned, and said unto Peter, Get thee behind Me, Satan: thou art an offence unto Me: for thou savourest not the things that be of God, but those that be of men."*

Mark 5:5-13 -- Jesus discerned that there was an *"unclean"* spirit in the man; that there was actually a whole legion. Again, this was done many times in the ministry of Christ. (See also Luke 9:42.)

Matthew 16:15-17 -- Jesus discerned that Peter's utterance was directly inspired by and revealed by God. It is a real caution to realize that the same man can speak at one time inspired by the Holy Spirit and at another time inspired by the wrong spirit.

* In the Old Testament prophets:

I Kings 22:23 -- *"Now therefore, behold the Lord hath put a lying spirit in the mouth of all these thy prophets, and the Lord hath spoken evil concerning thee."*

The prophet Micaiah saw the whole picture, from the heavenlies down to the spirit, which motivated the false prophets (I Kings 22:19-23).

II Kings 6:16-17 -- Elisha was able to see the angelic armies of the Lord surrounding them, and at his request, God opened the eyes of the young servant, enabling him to see these spirit beings as well.

* In the life of the New Testament leaders:

Acts 5:3 -- *"But Peter said, Ananias, why hath Satan filled thine heart to lie to the Holy Ghost, and to keep back part of the price of the land?"*

Peter not only operated in knowledge, wisdom and miracles, but also discerned their spirits.

Acts 8:21-23 -- *"Thou hast neither part nor lot in this matter: for thy heart is not right in the sight of God. Repent therefore of this thy wickedness, and pray God, if perhaps the thought of thine heart may be forgiven thee. For I perceive that thou art in the gall of bitterness, and in the bond of iniquity."*

Acts 13:9-10-- *"Then Saul, filled with the Holy Ghost, set his eyes on him, and said, O full of all subtilty and all mischief, thou child of the devil, thou enemy of all righteousness, wilt thou not cease to pervert the right ways of the Lord?"*

It is usually true that this gift works in close association with the gifts of knowledge, wisdom and faith. It may even involve the working of miracles. The gift may be given to one with a ministry of mercy and intercession, so that such a person might bear needs before the Lord in prayer on a high level, particularly relating to needs involving conditions of the human spirit. Along this line, notice that Scripture gives many different conditions of human spirits: a faith spirit (Proverbs 11:13); a hasty spirit (Proverbs 14:29); a perverse spirit (Proverbs 15:4); a broken spirit (Proverbs 15:13); a haughty spirit (Proverbs 16:18); a humble spirit (Proverbs 16:19; 29:23); an excellent spirit (Proverbs 17:27); a wounded spirit (Proverbs 18:14); an unruly or uncontrolled spirit (Proverbs 25:28). Discerning the human spirit is not only a matter of identifying into which of the three spirit realms it falls, but even the very condition of that spirit.

Notice the position of discerning of spirits in the list of the gifts. It is in the middle of the vocal gifts (prophecy, tongues and interpretation of tongues). This suggests that discernment is needed in that entire area so as to know which communications come from God and which come from the other sources. God will usually give this discernment to the pastor and true feeders of the flock so that they might be equipped to guide, guard and feed the flock.

Notice that Luke 9:1-2 and 10:2, 17-19 show that we need this gift in order to completely fulfill the commission of Christ. It is to go along with preaching the Gospel and healing the sick. If we are to effectively minister among the *"wolves,"* we must be able to discern who the *"wolves"* are (Acts 20:28-30). If we are to cast out evil spirits, we must first be able to discern them.

One general way of distinguishing between the discerning of spirits and the word of knowledge is that discerning of spirits has specifically to do with insight into the spirit realm: which spirit is at work and the very thoughts and motives of the heart. Discernment or perception of things outside the spirit realm is more the work of the words of knowledge or wisdom: events, circumstances, facts, etc.

20

What is the "Gift of Faith"?

We are now looking at the "power gifts." Just as with the utterance and revelation gifts, there are three (refer to beginning of Chapter 17). They are called power gifts because they are small expressions of the omnipotence of the Lord. Through these, God intervenes in nature wherever and whenever necessary to accomplish His divine will.

Studying the gifts of faith is not the same as studying the general subject of faith. Though the general subject of faith does relate to it and to a measure, helps our understanding of the gift of faith, there is still a marked difference. We will survey briefly the three kinds of faith, but let us define the gift of faith.

The gift of faith defined:

The gift of faith is the God-given ability to believe Him for the impossible in a particular situation. It is not so much the general faith which believes God for provision, but goes a step beyond, where one *just knows* that a particular thing is the will of God and is going to happen.

Again, we should point out the supernatural character of all these gifts. Through them, the Holy Spirit manifests and makes Himself visible or evident by His own activity.

This gift is specifically mentioned in I Corinthians 12:9, is referred to in I Corinthians 13:2, and may be included in the thought of I Corinthians 13:13. Besides these references, the gift of faith is illustrated and seen in its outworking and operation through the first five books of the New Testament.

What three kinds of faith are revealed in Scripture?

Any statement found in the Bible about, or characteristic of, faith falls into one of three categories:

* **Saving faith** -- John 1:12; Galatians 3:26; Ephesians 2:8.

This is that initial faith response to God which brings us into the Kingdom of God. It is God's enabling us to accept and believe in Him.

God's means of saving us was GRACE; our means of accepting it is FAITH.

Ephesians 2:8 -- *"For by grace are ye saved through faith; and that not of yourselves: it is the gift of God."*

The word "through" is very significant here. It is the Greek word *dia* and denotes the "channel of an act." It is a connecting thought, as water goes from one body to another *"through"* a channel. It speaks of a medium or route by which God's grace is transmitted to us. Faith is like an inlet (entrance) for all God's provision. As a dam that opens its inlets and allows water to pass through, our faith-response to God initially allows His grace to pour in and flood our souls, which is the new birth.

It is first *by* the agency or means of grace, then *through* faith that salvation comes. It is made possible and offered by grace, but must be accepted and received by faith. God prepared the provision by grace, and then offers it to us, at the same time working in our hearts to respond, imparting to us the ability to believe and receive. Yet He leaves a small gap which can only be spanned by our wills, responding and opening up to Him.

* **Faith as a *"fruit of the Spirit"*** -- Galatians 5:22; Acts 6:5, 8; 11:24; II Corinthians 4:13; Colossians 2:5.

Involved in the idea of fruit are gradual growth, seasons, external conditions and nourishment. We as individuals are as seeds which contain the inner germ of life, and as our outer shells die, the life within flourishes and produces fruit after its kind. Even after the fruit begins to appear, it must still ripen to maturity. It may be evident in many different stages of growth.

This speaks of faith as an attribute within our character and personality. Paul shows this as a developing factor in our lives. In Romans 1:17, he uses the phrase *"from faith to faith."* Righteousness is received by faith, and after it is received, it produces more faith in our lives, and we go on to live by faith.

As we look at this general aspect of faith, we see that it can either be wavering (James 1:6), or strong (Romans 4:20), or it may be anywhere in between. Scripture speaks about weak faith (Matthew 6:30; 16:8), temporary faith (Luke 8:13), unfeigned faith (I Timothy 1:5; II Timothy 1:5), great faith (Matthew 8:10) and unwavering faith (Hebrews 10:23; 11:6).

It should also be understood that faith, just as love, cannot stand alone. It is always connected with other virtues and qualities, such as patience (James 1:3; Hebrews 6:12), love (I Thessalonians 5:8; I Corinthians 13:13), hope (I Corinthians 13:13), power (II Thessalonians 1:11), good works (I Thessalonians 1:3), clear conscience (I Timothy 1:5), doctrinal soundness (Titus 1:13; 2:2), virtue (II Peter 1:5), knowledge (II Peter 1:6), importunity (Luke 11:5-10), joy (James 1:2-3; I Peter 1:6-8), good confession (Romans 10:9-10; Colossians 3:16-17).

To oversimplify faith and assume it to be only a crisis act of obedience has merit at a certain point. But if we believers are not taught a concept of faith broader than occasional acts of faith, we will be frustrated. Faith is presented in the Bible as a way of life. It is only as faith involves the proper blend of all the attributes mentioned that it is a living quality faith. Many Christians have only a crisis faith, rather than living a life of faith.

Romans 12:3 -- *"For I say, through the grace given unto me, to every man that is among you, not to think of himself more highly than he ought to think; but to think soberly, according as God hath dealt to every man the measure of faith."*

"Dealt" here means to divide into portions, as Joseph gave a portion of food to each of his brothers, but gave Benjamin five times as much (Genesis 43:16-34).

God gives to each of us a particular capacity to take in or respond to His gifts and grace, which He has designed for our general good. We are, therefore, each to function according to the proportion (measure) of faith God has given and enabled us to develop. Though we are all to have strong faith, when it comes to gifts and spiritual functions, this faith will be channeled and manifested in a variety of ways. We are all specialists in different areas. For instance, a transmission specialist could possibly install an air conditioner in an automobile, but not as effectively or efficiently as a specialist in air conditioning.

We must recognize this truth in order to understand body ministry function. We are all to receive from the strengths and gifts and measures of faith God has placed in each of us. In addition, it is not proper to try to operate at a level of faith that is *"beyond our measure"* (II Corinthians 10:12-16).

It is not right to try to require conformity of each member, or to make demands on a person that go beyond his measure of faith. To violate the sphere and scope of one's ministry will frustrate him. This is not to say that a degree of frustration may accompany God's enlarging of one's ministry into new areas and dimensions.

* The gift of faith -- I Corinthians 12:9; 13:2

We suggest that this gift involves two general levels: (1) faith to function in individual ministries as is mentioned in Romans 12:3-8 and, (2) faith for specific miracles or acts which God would perform in given circumstances (I Corinthians 12:9).

It is difficult to differentiate dogmatically between the fruit of faith and the gift of faith. It seems in practical life and ministry that the Lord imparts faith to us for our particular ministries. We have a level of faith in those areas which is absolute and unwavering. Each of us knows our ministry and believes God to honor it and prosper it at all times.

But going on from there, let us deal with what is probably the clearest and purest level spoken of in Scripture as the gift of faith.

Mark 11:22-24 -- *"And Jesus answering saith unto them, Have faith in God. For verily I say unto you, That whosoever shall say unto this mountain, Be thou removed, and be thou cast into the sea; and shall not doubt in his heart, but shall believe that those things which he saith shall come to pass; he shall have whatsoever he saith. Therefore I say unto you, What things soever ye desire, when ye pray, believe that ye receive them, and ye shall have them."*

Jesus tells us that it is faith which leaves absolutely no doubt in the heart of the one believing. The word used for *"ask"* is the same as the word for *"take."* It is not in question form, rather implies an active receiving of the known will of God.

The gift of faith illustrated:

In the life of Christ

Matthew 8:1-3 -- Jesus did not display any shade of doubt concerning the healing of this leper. The words Jesus spoke to him as He touched him were, *"I will; be thou clean."* We see in these words absolute faith.

John 11:11 -- Jesus knew that He was going to a dead man. Lazarus had already died, but Jesus said He would *"awake him out of sleep."*

John 9:1-7 -- Jesus knew that this man, who had been blind from birth, was going to be healed so that the works of God might be made manifest -- absolute faith in an act which had not yet happened.

To these could be added a multitude of examples from the life of Christ. His life was literally filled with the manifestation of absolute faith.

In the lives of the Apostles

Acts 3:1-7 -- Peter proclaimed this man's healing with unflinching and unwavering faith, then took him by the hand and lifted him to his feet.

Acts 5:1-10 -- Peter fearlessly tells both Ananias and Sapphira what God is about to do to them.

Acts 13:8-11 -- Paul received divinely imparted faith to know what was to happen to Elymas the sorcerer. Immediately after he spoke, Elymas was smitten blind.

Acts 16:16-18 -- Paul took absolute authority over the evil spirit in this young woman and commanded it to come out. It came out *"the same hour."*

Acts 20:7-12 -- A young man of Troas fell from the third story and was taken up dead. Paul went through a procedure similar to that used by Elijah and prayed for the boy. He then told the people not to be troubled; the boy would live.

Acts 27:21-25 -- Paul gave a word of faith to the crew in a storm-tossed ship, assuring them that none would perish.

What key factor recurs over and over in the gift of faith?

The gift of faith rests on knowing the will of God. This may come by special revelation, such as dreams, visions; it may come by the inner voice of the Spirit; or by the written Word of God, quickened for specific direction. It operates on the same principle as all faith: *"Faith cometh by hearing, and hearing by the Word of God"* (Romans 10:17). The sure knowledge of His will produces absolute faith: *"This is the confidence that we have in Him, that, if we ask any thing according to His will, He heareth us"* (I John 5:14).

The gift of faith is dependent on the gift of knowledge. They are mingled inseparably. When God reveals certain facts concerning His will in a circumstance, one *"just knows"* it will happen. This is an irresistible, unshakable faith. He then acts accordingly. It may be for the working of miracles, meeting physical or financial needs, healings, reconciliation of relationships.

Notice this principle in the *"faith chapter"* of Hebrews 11:

vs 7 -- Noah acted in faith at the word of God concerning the flood.

vs 8 -- Abraham's going out was on the basis of God's word to him.

vs 11 -- Sarah believed she could bear a child because of the word spoken to her by the Lord.

vs 30 -- Israel compassed the walls of Jericho by faith because of the revealed will of God.

We should note that the gift of faith often operates in connection with several other gifts. It often operates with the gifts of miracles and healings. It nearly always involves a word of knowledge, and at times even a word of wisdom and discerning of spirits. It may also involve prophecy.

The gift of faith should be among the *"best gifts"* (I Corinthians 12:30), mainly because it greatly edifies when it functions in proper balance, and blends with the plurality of ministry, and, is not used to exalt self. God has placed no limitation on how much faith we can have. Though we are given a *"measure,"* we can cause that to grow to any proportion which we are able to receive (Romans 12:3).

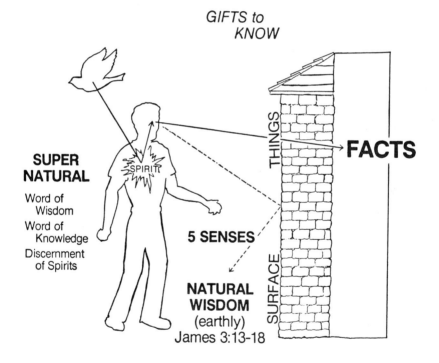

GIFTS to
KNOW

SUPER
NATURAL

Word of
Wisdom
Word of
Knowledge
Discernment
of Spirits

SPIRIT

THINGS

FACTS

5 SENSES

SURFACE

NATURAL
WISDOM
(earthly)
James 3:13-18

21

What are the "Gifts of Healing"?

How could the gifts of healing best be defined?

The gift of healing is the God-given ability to impart healing to the physical body at specific times. It is accompanied by a measure of the gift of faith, and often, the gift of knowledge. It involves the impartation of that faith to the one who needs healing, lifting him out of the realm of doubt and unbelief, and taking appropriate steps toward healing. It is a *"manifestation of the Spirit"* (I Corinthians 12:7) through a person and not just his own powers of persuasion.

Why is it the gifts of healing (plural), instead of the gift of healing (singular)?

We notice that in each case where healing is referred to as a gift of the Spirit in ministry, it is always in the plural form:

I Corinthians 12:9 -- *"Gifts of healings. . ."*

I Corinthians 12:28 -- *"Gifts of healings. . ."*

I Corinthians 12:30 -- *"Gifts of healing. . ."*

It is the only gift which uses the plural in this way. This indicates that the gift of healing may operate on more than one level. It could refer to the fact that different kinds of sicknesses require different kinds of healings and various levels of faith. Some healings, for example, may involve underlying attitudes which must be dealt with before the body will respond. Other healings need an outright miracle.

Some healings are instantaneous and others are gradual.

It is a matter of observation that one person may be used to bring healing in a specialized area. For example, one may have faith for the healing of blindness, another deafness, another cancer.

This makes it all the more important to realize that Jesus had power over *"all manner of sickness and all manner of disease"* (Matthew 10:1). God gave Him not the Spirit *"by measure,"* but in *"fullness"* (Colossians 1:19). Jesus gave the twelve disciples (collectively) power over *"all manner of sickness and all manner of disease."*

The measure of healing brought through ministry relates directly to our level of faith. Faith must operate in the gifts of healing since the different ministries of healing are actually specialty areas of faith. Though all may pray for the sick (Mark 16:17-18), I Corinthians 12:28-30 indicates that some of us are used more in healing than others.

What levels of healings do we see in the Scriptures?

* **Instantaneous** -- Some healings are of a simple physical nature and the necessary work of the Holy Spirit can be done immediately.

   Matthew 8:3 -- *"And Jesus put forth His hand, and touched him, saying, I will; be thou clean. And immediately his leprosy was cleansed."*

   Mark 1:31 -- *"And He came and took her by the hand, and lifted her up; and immediately the fever left her, and she ministered unto them."*

* **Gradual** -- It might be said that man has three main areas which need healing or divine health and soundness; the spirit, the soul, and the body.

There may be cases where the body is sick because of

inner sickness of the soul or spirit. The Lord may choose to heal by healing the attitude of the heart, with physical healing becoming gradually evident as the inner problem is solved. Therefore, it may often be necessary for a person with a gift of healing to also have the gifts of discernment and knowledge in order to understand the dealings of God in each life. This principle is alluded to in I Corinthians 11:27-34 within the context of the communion table. Some had inner problems and were violating the Lord's body. They were said to be weak and sickly, and some had even died as a direct result of this. To just pray a prayer of faith over them was not sufficient. They needed spiritual illumination and understanding, and the correction of their sin of *"not discerning the Lord's body."*

James 5:14-16 also implies that there may be a connection between sin and sickness; that part of the healing process is to confess our faults.

III John 2 -- *"Beloved, I wish above all things that thou mayest prosper and be in health, even as thy soul prospereth."*

(See also Isaiah 1:5; Jeremiah 8:22; Mark 2:17; Psalm 41:4; Isaiah 53:5; Luke 4:18.)

Even apart from this realm of gradual healing, there may be some predominantly physical healing cases which take place gradually. In John 4:52 the nobleman's son was healed by the word of Jesus without His actual presence. The man inquired of his servants the next day when his son *"began to amend."*

Mark 8:22-25 -- In most cases where Jesus prayed for people there was instant and miraculous healing. But in this case, healing came in two stages. As the principle of gradual healing worked in the ministry of Christ to some degree, we should also expect to see it work in our own healing ministries to an even greater degree (John 14:12).

NOTE: Even Paul recognized that, in cases where there are emotional or attitude problems which are causing psychosomatic symptoms and physical problems, it was not just a matter of praying for the symptoms. He recommended that Timothy take a little wine for medicinal purposes. He did not reject the idea of using medicine or natural healing methods in such cases. Often these may be the means we should use for temporary relief. But Paul also worked on bringing Timothy to a higher level of maturity and faith, which would in itself bring him physical relief.

Through what methods did healing operate in the Scriptures?

* **Calling for the elders and anointing with oil --**

James 5:14-15 -- *"Is any sick among you? let him call for the elders of the church; and let them pray over him, anointing him with oil in the name of the Lord: and the prayer of faith shall save the sick, and the Lord shall raise him up; and if he have committed sins, they shall be forgiven him."*

The oil is a representation of the Holy Spirit. It is not the oil that healed through medicinal qualities, but *"the prayer of faith shall save the sick."*

* **The communion --** (I Corinthians 11:27-34) -- The clear implication is that there is a level of healing in the proper *"discerning of the Lord's body,"* which is not available from any other source. We enter into harmony and unity, love and proper relatedness, in one body.

I Corinthians 11:29-30 -- *"For he that eateth and drinketh unworthily, eateth and drinketh damnation to himself, not discerning the Lord's body. For this cause many are weak* *and sickly among you, and many sleep."*

God has, to a large degree, bound our physical well-being to our ability to relate spiritually to the *"flesh"* and *"bone"* aspect of Christ (Ephesians 5:30).

* **Laying on of hands and prayer by believers** -- (Mark 16:16-18; Matthew 19:13-15) -- God has not limited His provisions to one means or through only a select few. He will use whomever is available and will believe Him. We all have as our prerogative to believe God's Word and pray for the sick.

* **By the spoken word** -- (Luke 7:1-10) -- There were three kinds of people that came to Jesus for healing:

   (1) Those who came for healing personally;

   (2) Those who brought someone else for healing;

   (3) Those who came for someone else, and sought only the word of Jesus stating they would be healed; they saw no barrier in time and space.

Jesus said that this third level was the greatest level of faith. This does not mean, however, that the other methods are not valid. There is a real ministry in bringing the sick to those who have faith, and at times, there may be a real need to call for the elders.

* **By the touch of a garment, or the shadow of the disciple-**

Mark 6:56 -- *"And whithersoever he entered, into villages, or cities, or country, they laid the sick in the streets, and besought Him that they might touch if it were but the border of His garment: and as many as touched Him were made whole."*

Acts 5:15-16 -- *"Insomuch that they brought forth the sick into the streets, and laid them on beds and couches, that at least the shadow of Peter passing by might overshadow some* *of them. There came also a multitude out of the cities round about unto Jerusalem, bringing sick folks, and them which were vexed with unclean spirits: and they were healed every one."*

It is on the basis of faith that we are healed. Faith underlies the entire truth of healing. Faith is required from the one in need and the one praying and even from those who bring the sick (Matthew 9:2).

* **Handkerchiefs and aprons from Paul --**

Acts 19:11-12 -- *"And God wrought special miracles by the hands of Paul: so that from his body were brought unto the sick handkerchiefs or aprons, and the diseases departed from them, and the evil spirits went out of them."*

Notice, these are called *"special miracles."* Incidents of this type have happened even in modern days, but they are not the norm. They were done this way because there was no other way for Paul to contact them.

How do we know if we have the gifts of healing?

* **By the inner witness of the Spirit --**

Ephesians 3:16 -- *"That he would grant you, according to the riches of His glory, to be strengthened with might by His Spirit in the inner man."*

(See also Romans 8:16; Hebrews 10:15; I John 5:6.)

* **By the ability to believe God for physical healing --** Paul taught in Romans 12:3-8 that we each have different spiritual abilities and grace levels given us by the Lord. With each function comes a proportionate *"measure of faith"* (vs. 3) to see God accomplish His work.

This can also be seen in I Corinthians 12:27-31. The very fact that we have a variety of functions indicates that we have varying faith channeled in various directions.

* **Through compassion for sick and afflicted** -- There will be a constant and deep concern on one's heart. And not only a concern, but a desire also to do something about it. There will be a mobility and a strength of faith behind this compassion.

Over and over it is said Jesus had compassion on those who were sick and suffering. This was largely what motivated Him to heal them.

Matthew 20:34 -- compassion on two blind men.

Mark 1:41 -- compassion on the leper.

Luke 7:12-14 -- compassion on the widow; raised her dead son.

* **By results** -- The test of any ministry or gifts is the fruit it bears. If one has the gifts of healing, then people will be healed. Of course, the results will develop and increase with the spiritual growth of the person having the gift.

* **By the demands being placed upon you by others** -- Wherever there is a gift of ministry, there will be a response from others in regard to that area. This gradually produces a demand upon the person with the gift. All one need do is function as the Lord leads and He will make room for ministry (Proverbs 18:16). On the other hand, if it is only a human ambition and desire not birthed of the Holy Spirit, that person will have to promote it himself and even then others will not respond because it does not bear fruit (Proverbs 25:14).

* **By the laying on of hands of the presbytery (elders)** -- Many times gifts and ministries are enunciated and clearly spoken through prophetic ministry; establishing our place of ministry in the local church. Paul frequently brought to Timothy's attention the stewardship he had of the

ministry spoken over him in this manner (I Timothy 1:18; 4:14; II Timothy 1:6).

What is the purpose of the gifts of healing?

* **God loves His people and wants them to be in good health** -- referring to total health to the body, soul and spirit. God so loved that He "gave." There is no end to what God desires to give us as an inheritance in the Kingdom (III John 2-4).

* **Divine health and healing are aspects of the rectifying of the curse of the law --**

  I John 3:8 -- *"For this purpose the son of God was manifested, that He might destroy the works of the devil."*

  Galatians 3:13-14 -- *"Christ hath redeemed us from the curse of the law, being made a curse for us: for it is written, Cursed is every one that hangeth on a tree: that the blessing of Abraham might come on the Gentiles through Jesus Christ; that we might receive the promise of the Spirit through faith."*

  Redemption involves bringing men totally out of the effects of the curses involved in the law, which includes sickness and disease.

* **To confirm our message with signs and wonders (Hebrews 2:3-4)** -- It was a part of the great commission (Mark 16:15-20).

  John 5:36 -- *"...the same works that I do, bear witness of Me, that the Father hath sent Me."*

What is the source of sickness?

* **Satan** -- (Acts 10:38) -- Jesus came to heal all that were

"oppressed of the devil."

Actually, it could be said that all disease and sickness has its source in Satan and his evil influence; he is the source of all disease, germ and harmful bacteria. This can be traced back to the very beginning and observed throughout history. The influence of Satan over people is what brings them sickness and disease. After the fall, sickness and disease came to both man's physical being and his spiritual nature.

* **Sin** -- Physical sickness is really produced by spiritual sickness. When man's soul becomes corrupted by sin, his body becomes subject to sickness and disease as a consequence.

Deuteronomy 28:58-61 -- *"If thou wilt not observe to do all the words of this law that are written in this book, that thou mayest fear this glorious and fearful name, THY LORD THY GOD; then the Lord will make thy plagues wonderful, and the plagues of thy seed, even great plagues, and of long continuance, and sore sicknesses, and of long continuance. Moreover he will bring upon thee all the diseases of Egypt, which thou wast afraid of; and they shall cleave unto thee. Also every sickness, and every plague, which is not written in the book of this law, them will the Lord bring upon thee, until thou be destroyed."*

On what basis are believers healed?

* **Redemption** -- Physical healing, as well as spiritual healing, was included in the atoning work of Christ and brought out constantly by both the Old Testament and New Testament. Note these statements in regard to the deliverance of Israel from Egypt:

Exodus 15:25-26 -- *"There He made for them a statute and an ordinance, and there He proved them, and said, If thou wilt diligently hearken to the voice of the Lord thy God, and wilt do that which is right in His sight, and wilt give ear to*

His commandments, and keep all His statutes, I will put none of these diseases upon thee, which I have brought upon the Egyptians: for I am the Lord that healeth thee."

This was an actual part of God's covenant with Israel. Sickness belonged to the Egyptians (sinners), not to God's people who knew His delivering power and walked in covenant with Him.

Psalm 105:37 -- *"He brought them forth also with silver and gold: and there was not one feeble person among their tribes."*

Psalm 103:2-3 -- *"Bless the Lord, O my soul, and forget not all His benefits: who forgiveth all thine iniquities; who healeth all thy diseases."*

Isaiah 53:4-5 -- *"Surely He hath borne our griefs, and carried our sorrows: yet we did esteem Him stricken, smitten of God, and afflicted. But He was wounded for our transgressions, He was bruised for our iniquities: the chastisement of our peace was upon Him; and with His stripes we are healed."*

Matthew 8:16-17 -- *"He healed all that were sick: that it might be fulfilled which was spoken by Isaiah the prophet, saying, Himself took our infirmities, and bare our sicknesses."*

III John 2 -- *"Beloved, I wish above all things that thou mayest prosper and be in health, even as thy soul prospereth."*

These and many other Scriptures show us that our redemption was not only spiritual, but physical also. Just as He removes sin from us, He also desires to remove sickness from us.

When Jesus healed, He often also forgave sin. He linked sickness within, and forgave the sin before He healed. The two are tied together by James.

James 5:15 -- *"And the prayer of faith shall save the sick, and the Lord shall rise him up; and if he have committed sins, they shall be forgiven him."*

(See also I Peter 2:24; Romans 5:12.)

* Faith -- Jesus ministered to people according to their faith.

Matthew 9:2 -- *"...and Jesus seeing their faith said unto the sick of the palsy..."*

Matthew 9:22 -- *"...thy faith hath made thee whole. And the woman was made whole from that hour."*

Matthew 9:29 -- *"Then touched He their eyes saying, According to your faith be it unto you."*

Luke 18:42 -- *"And Jesus said unto him, Receive thy sight: thy faith hath saved thee."*
II Corinthians 5:7 -- *"We walk by faith, not by sight."*

This means we agree with the Word, accept it unto our personal lives, and act upon it.

Mark 11:24 -- *"Therefore I say unto you, What things soever ye desire, when ye pray, believe that ye receive them, and ye shall have them."*

Faith is to be based solely on the Word of God. Romans 10:17 says, *"So then faith cometh by hearing, and hearing by the Word of God."*

(See also Hebrews 10:23; Isaiah 55:11; Revelation 12:11; Matthew 4:4-11.)

22

What is the "Gift of Miracles"?

Miracles defined:

A miracle is a happening or event which is supernatural; the performance of something which is against the laws of nature. A miracle could be called a supernatural phenomenon. Miracles defy reason and transcend natural laws.

The one thing which makes Christianity unique is the supernatural. Christianity is totally based on the supernatural. The gift of miracles is simply the God-given ability to cooperate with God as He performs miracles. It is actually a co-action, or a joint operation; man participating with God in the performing of the impossible. It is not man performing miracles, but God performing miracles through a cooperative act with men (I Corinthians 12:10,28).

The word *"miracle"* in I Corinthians 12:10 is from the Greek word *dunamis.* It speaks of God's energy or power, ability or might. It is translated *"power"* 77 times, *"mighty work"* 11 times, *"miracle"* 7 times, *"might"* 4 times, *"mighty"* 2 times, and *"virtue"* 3 times, plus several other miscellaneous ways in the King James version of the Bible.

The place and importance of miracles:

Miracles are a major theme of the Bible. Miraculous manifestations always accompanied Jesus. They also accompanied His disciples. They are to accompany us also because they are a part of the *"good news"* (Gospel). Without the miraculous, we have an incomplete Gospel. We can only testify of Christ as we display the supernatural in our lives (John 5:36). His works must accompany His Word. Notice how the Gospel was spread in the early church.

Hebrews 2:4 - *"God also bearing them witness, both with signs and wonders, and with divers miracles, and gifts of the Holy Ghost, according to His own will."*

Some Christians and theologians believe that the age of miracles is past. Others imply that God saves and indwells men, and that this produces a miraculous revolution in their lives and attitudes.

Yet we cannot relegate God to the realm of performing the miraculous only in the hearts of men. We need both the internal and the external experiences of God's power. And it is the will of God to manifest Himself in both realms. Notice both these being brought out in the following Scripture references:

Internal -- Ephesians 1:17-19; 3:16, 20; Philippians 3:10; Colossians 1:11.

External -- Acts 1:8; 3:12; 4:7; 4:33; 6:8; 8:10; Mark 16:17-20; John 14:12-14.

Some argue that we have the Scriptures and do not need miracles. The statement Jesus made to the Sadducees could apply here: *"Ye do err, not knowing the Scriptures, nor the power of God"* (Matthew 22:29). Not only do we need the word, but the power of God as well. Paul tells the Thessalonians that the Gospel came not only in word, but in power (I Thessalonians 1:5).

Without the miraculous the Word cannot be fulfilled, for it is a part of His Word. Paul speaks of those who have only a form of godliness (likeness), but lack the power (dunamis) (II Timothy 3:5).

The place of the miraculous is therefore as fundamental to Christianity as is the new birth. It is an integral part of the New Covenant.

Miracles are governed by the will of God and obedience of man:

* **Hearing the word of God** -- There must first be a communication of the mind and will of God. This is illustrated in Scripture over and over again. Here are only a few illustrations:

Ezekiel 37:1-10 -- The Lord first told the prophet what he was to say to the dry bones. He acted on that basis, *"So I prophesied as I was commanded..."*

Exodus 14:16 -- Moses stretched out his rod in direct obedience to the word of the Lord and the Red Sea opened. Most of Moses' ministry consisted of obeying God and seeing miracles take place.

Acts 14:8-11 -- We note that Paul beheld this man for some time and perception came to Paul that he had faith to be healed.

Scripture bears out the fact that God almost always works miracles in connection with man, not independently of man. Though a miracle is, in a sense, a sovereign act of God, it also involves communicating His will to men and involving them in it.

Jesus did only that which He was directed by the Father to do.

John 5:17, 19-20 -- *"But Jesus answered them, My Father worketh hitherto, and I work...Then answered Jesus and said unto them, Verily, verily, I say unto you, The Son can do nothing of Himself, but what He seeth the Father do: for what things soever He doeth, these also doeth the Son likewise. For the Father loveth the Son, and sheweth Him all things that Himself doeth: and He will shew Him greater* *works than these, that ye may marvel."*

* Believe the Word -- Faith could be simply defined as an act of obedience. It becomes necessary for God's men to obey what He reveals to them. For example, the Old Testament prophets not only received the word of the Lord, but they accepted it, believed it, and actually staked their lives on it.

Mark 11:23 -- *"For verily I say unto you, That whosoever shall say unto this mountain, Be thou removed, and be thou cast into the sea; and shall not doubt in his heart, but shall believe that those things which he saith shall come to pass; he shall have whatsoever he saith."*

Acts 13:9-12 -- Though this is an example of a negative or judgmental miracle, notice the attitude of faith and confidence, in which Paul operated. There is no hint of doubt in the tone of Paul's words.

* Speaking the word -- In the first chapter of Genesis we observe that involved in each creative act is the statement, *"and God said."* All creation was the product of His spoken, creative word. Hebrews 1:3 tells us that He is *"upholding"* (sustaining) all things by the word (uttered word) of His power. His spoken word is the means God uses to release His power. He speaks things into existence.

Psalm 33:6 -- *"By the word of the Lord were the heavens made; and all the host of them by the breath of His mouth."*

Whenever God desires to perform a miracle, He seeks an instrument through which He can speak or articulate His word. Jesus Christ was the instrument through which He spoke the world into existence (Hebrews 1:2). In fact, Christ is said to have been the Word of God personified (John 1:1-2). This principle can be traced throughout the Bible. Notice the spoken word in the following references:

John 5:8 -- *"Jesus saith unto him, Rise, take up thy bed, and walk. And immediately the man was made whole."*

John 11:43, 44 -- *"And when He had thus spoken, He cried with a loud voice, Lazarus come forth. And he that was dead came forth."*

Acts 3:6 -- *"Then Peter said, Silver and gold have I none; but such as a I have give I thee: In the name of Jesus Christ of Nazareth rise up and walk."*

(See also John 6:63; Matthew 8:8; Romans 4:17; Jeremiah 1:12.)

* **Acting on the word** -- There are often acts of faith which must accompany the speaking of the word.

James 2:17 -- *"Even so faith, if it hath not works, is dead, being alone."*

Acts 20:9-10 -- After Eutychus was killed by falling out the window, Paul performed an act of faith by lying on him and embracing him, then he was brought back to life.

NOTE: This whole section on the will of God and the obedience of man can be illustrated by the story of the man of God crying out against the altar at Bethel, and the signs that followed his prophecy (I Kings 13:1-5). Also notice the story of Elijah offering his memorable sacrifice to God in I Kings 18:36-38.

What are the purposes of miracles?

* **For deliverance and preservation** -- This is based on the love and compassion of the Lord toward His people. Ten times in the Gospels, it is said that prior to performing miracles for the people, Christ was moved with compassion (Mark 1:41).

All the miracles and plagues in Egypt were for the deliverance and preservation of Israel. This is also true of the miraculous provision made for Israel while in the wilderness. The greatest epoch of miracles in all recorded history was during the lives and ministries of Jesus and the Apostles. They were a sign of God's love and covenant relationship with His people.

* **For the edification and building up of faith** -- The manifested power of God always causes men to stand in awe and have a healthy fear of God. To honor and respect and fear God is essential for the well-being and faith of all of us. Proverbs 1:7 tells us that the fear of the Lord is the beginning of knowledge. It is upon this kind of knowledge that faith is built.

Notice even in the negative example of Ananias and Sapphira, God's power resulted in great fear coming upon all the church (Acts 5:11).

John 2:11 -- *"This beginning of miracles did Jesus in Cana of Galilee, and manifested forth His glory; and His disciples believed on Him."*

John 20:30-31 -- *"And many other signs truly did Jesus in the presence of His disciples, which are not written in this book: but these are written that ye might believe that Jesus is the Christ, the Son of God; and that believing ye might have life through His name."*

The miracles Jesus performed validated His message and His identity. We should make it clear that miracles are not designed to appease the curiosity of the hard-hearted and unbelieving. Jesus told the sign-seeking Jews that no sign would be given them except that of the prophet Jonah. So, our point is here that for believers who are already His disciples, miracles increase our faith. Miracles are not so much designed to give us faith initially, but once we have faith, miracles aid in its growth.

(See also Psalm 103:1-7; Acts 8:5-8; John 16:24.)

* Miracles are to accompany the preaching of the Gospel and work in connection with evangelism -- Jesus attracted crowds as he performed miracles. The disciples after Him also operated this way. The miracle of the outpouring of the Spirit on the day of Pentecost resulted in the salvation of three thousand souls. Paul mentions in I Corinthians 14:22 that tongues are still a sign to unbelievers; an evidence of the supernatural. When tongues are practiced properly, they show the presence of God.

Mark 16:15-20 -- Miracles were a part of the commission to preach the Gospel.

All we have to do is follow the ministry of the New Testament apostles to see the important part miracles play in the advance of the Gospel.

The gift of miracles has not yet been fully restored to the church in the same measure as the other gifts. Revelation 11:5 seems to indicate that miracles will again operate on a large scale just prior to the coming of the Lord. The two witnesses mentioned seem to refer to the spirits of Elijah and Moses (Matthew 17:3-4) resting on the last day church. This is especially significant when one recalls that there were, in the history of the world, three major miracle epochs and that they were all represented on the Mount of Transfiguration; Moses in the wilderness; the era of Elijah and the accompanying miracles; and perhaps the greatest of them all, the ministry of Christ Himself.

Mark 9:23 -- *"Jesus said unto him, If thou canst believe, all things are possible to him that believeth."*

John 14:12-14 -- *"Verily, verily, I say unto you, He that believeth on Me, the works that I do shall he do also; and greater works than these shall he do; because I go unto My Father. And whatsoever ye shall ask in My name, that will I do, that the Father may be glorified in the Son. If ye ask any thing in My name, I will do it."*

When we believe the message of Christ, and miracles are

wrought, then is the Father indeed being glorified in and through the Son.

The need in the church is to believe and contend for this gift. As we have shown in this chapter, the gift is dependent on the sovereignty of God and the faith and obedience of man. In a day when we can expect God to move it is important that God's people open their hearts in faith and obedience and contend for the miraculous in the church today.

(See also Matthew 21:21-22; Mark 11:22-24; 16:15-20; John 15:7, 16.)

23

What is the "Gift of Prophecy"?

How may the gift of prophecy be defined?

The gift of prophecy is speaking under the direct supernatural influence of the Holy Spirit. It is becoming God's mouthpiece, to verbalize His words as the Spirit directs. The word *"prophecy"* used in I Corinthians 12:10, is the Greek word *propheteia,* and means "speaking forth the mind and counsel of God." It is inseparable in its New Testament usage with the concept of direct inspiration of the Spirit.

Revelation 19:10 -- *"For the testimony of Jesus is the spirit of prophecy."*

Prophecy is the very voice of Christ speaking in the church.

Jeremiah 33:11 -- *"...the voice of the Bridegroom, and the voice of the bride..."*

This Scripture depicts Christ speaking to His bride, the church. Prophecy is the very voice of Christ speaking to His people.

Is prophecy different than preaching?

There is no warrant for translating the word *propheteia* as preaching, teaching, or exhorting in a manner that robs it of its direct supernaturalness. The Scriptures do not confuse and interchange these words. There are different words used for preaching, teaching, or exhorting.

In the Scriptures, prophesying bore the very obvious earmark of a supernatural operation. We are not left at all with the impression that it was a natural preaching talent or teaching ability. Notice the emphasis on the supernaturalness of prophecy in the following verses:

I Timothy 4:1 -- *"Now the Spirit speaketh expressly..."*

Acts 2:11 -- *"Thus saith the Holy Ghost..."*

Luke 1:67 -- *"And his father Zacharias was filled with the Holy Ghost, and prophesied, saying..."*

Preaching may contain prophecy, but is not itself prophecy. On the other hand, prophecy is never to become a substitute for preaching and teaching; this was never its intended use.

Is prophecy valid for our day?

The New Testament refers about thirty times to prophecy and prophesying as a continuing part of the church.

In Joel 2:28, it was prophesied that there would be prophecy in our days. This was confirmed by Peter on the day of Pentecost (Acts 2:16-18).

I Corinthians 12:10, 28-29 shows us it is one of the gifts of the Spirit given to bring a spiritual body together as real functioning organs.

I Corinthians 13:9-10 -- *"For we know in part, and we prophesy in part. But when that which is perfect is come, then that which is in part shall be done away."*

Prophecy will be with us until Christ returns, according to this Scripture.

Romans 12:3-6 -- *"For I say, through the grace given unto me, to every man that is among you, not to think of himself more* *highly than he ought to think; but to think soberly, according as God hath dealt to every man the measure of faith. For as we have many members in one body, and all members have not the same office: so we, being many, are one body in Christ, and every one members one of another. Having then gifts differing according to the grace that is given to us, whether prophecy, let us prophesy according to the proportion of faith."*

Paul, by the Spirit, told the Thessalonians to *"quench not the Spirit. Despise not prophesyings"* (I Thessalonians 5:19-20). This is a timeless exhortation and should be taken to heart in our day.

Is there a difference between the written prophecies of the Bible and prophecy that is spoken today?

The prophecy of the Bible is a higher level of prophecy and will never be equaled or surpassed. It was given by God for the purpose of becoming His authoritative, inscripturated Word for the entire church age (II Peter 1:21; Ephesians 2:20).

The two great excesses of history relating to prophecy have been, on the one hand, to lift it to a point of infallibility, and on the other hand, to despise it. While we dare not give it too great authority and over focus on it, neither do we dare reduce it to the natural powers of man or do away with it altogether.

All spoken prophetic utterances today are to be judged by the Word and subject to it.

Deuteronomy 4:2 -- *"Ye shall not add unto the word which I command you, neither shall ye diminish ought from it..."*

Proverbs 30:6 -- *"Add thou not unto His words, lest He reprove thee, and thou be found a liar."*

Revelation 22:18-19 -- *"For I testify unto every man that* *heareth the words of the prophecy of this book, If any man shall add unto these things, God shall add unto him the plagues that are written in this book: and if any man shall take away from the words of the book of this prophecy, God shall take away his part out of the book of life..."*

What are the present purposes of prophecy?

✦ **Edification** -- *"He that prophesieth speaketh unto men to edification"* (I Corinthians 13:3). This is an architectural word speaking of building, erecting, or putting stones into place. This is one means God has provided whereby we may build up the church. It is vital that we build with quality materials (gifts, ministries) instead of wood, hay and stubble (I Corinthians 3:10-15).

* **Exhortation** -- I Corinthians 14:3 -- To exhort is to encourage, to advise and warn earnestly. Many times prophecies contain strong urging and earnest admonition. This often is the very mood and attitude of God being spoken to His people along a given line. It makes a strong impression on those who have ears to hear.

This is illustrated in Hoses 6:1-3. The people were exhorted regarding their direction: they must *"return."* They were told what their direction had produced. They were told what changes were needed and what it would produce.

The entire chapter of I Timothy 4 also illustrates this type of prophetic utterance.

* **Comfort** -- The Greek word used in I Corinthians 14:3 for comfort literally means speaking closely to anyone. It denotes consolation and comfort with a greater degree of tenderness than other Greek words for comfort (Vine's).

The prophetic word is Christ, not only drawing near and speaking, but speaking in great personal concern, tenderness and care. This is a great comfort. It not only makes us aware that He is there and speaking, but that He speaks with great intimacy and concern. (See Psalm 23:4; 119:50, 76; Ephesians 6:22.)

* To convict and convince -- This relates to believers who are unlearned as well as to unbelievers.

I Corinthians 14:24-25 -- *"But if all prophesy, and there come in one that believeth not, or one unlearned, he is convinced of all, he is judged of all: and thus are the secrets of his heart made manifest; and so falling down on his face, he will worship God, and report that God is in you of a truth."*

* For instruction and learning --

I Corinthians 14:31 -- *"For ye may all prophesy one by one, that all may learn, and all may be comforted."*

Though much of the recorded prophecy of Scripture was predictive, much of the message was for the purpose of communicating the current disposition and will of God toward His people. In fact, the root meaning of prophecy is not so much *"foretelling"* as it is *"forth-telling."* Prophecy is not therefore foretelling future events. It is God's way of communicating to His people. In the New Testament prophecy was primarily concerned with the domestic life of the church and not so much with the world.

There were various levels or degrees of inspiration and authority in prophetic utterances. The message of a prophet, for example, would usually carry a greater unction and authority than one from a member of the congregation who prophesied for edification or comfort. It is also a general principle that among the cross-section of those who prophesy some have a greater authority by virtue of their personal knowledge of God and overall maturity. For example, Moses spoke with greater authority than did the seventy elders who prophesied (Numbers 11:25-29).

Special mention should be made concerning prophecy for

the establishing and imparting of ministry (See I Timothy 1:18). Here Paul told young Timothy to wear prophecies as armor and go to war. This is a very important level of prophecy, and should be entered into only by qualified elders and with the greatest of precaution. It is too big a topic to be pursued in this study.

What are some of the different ways prophecy may come to a person and be expressed?

* Prophecies may come:

As spontaneous utterances -- something revealed on the spot that is totally unpremeditated and comes from the Spirit within. While nothing is actually seen or heard, strong impressions or thoughts flood from the spirit of the man and fill his mind (I Corinthians 2:9-16). These thoughts are then spoken in the meeting in a timely manner.

Through visions -- this may be more in the realm of the prophet's ministry, though it could happen to anyone. (Ananias is an example -- Acts 9:10-16). This was a common experience for the Old Testament prophets (Isaiah 6; Revelation 1; Numbers 24).

Through dreams and night visions -- (Daniel 7; Genesis 37:5-9; Numbers 12:6; Joel 2).

Through an angel -- (Revelation 1:1; Acts 10:22; 27:23-25).

* Prophecies may be expressed or delivered:

By simply speaking or verbalizing -- under the unction of the Holy Spirit (I Corinthians 14:4, 6, 19).

Through demonstrative actions -- acting them out in a parable-like or figurative form. This seems to be almost exclusively in the realm of the ministry of a prophet (I Samuel 15:26-28; Acts 21:10-11).

Through writing them down -- many of the prophecies of the Old Testament were given in advance to the time they were delivered or written. Again, this seems to relate to a higher level of prophecy than that which comes from the general congregation for edification, exhortation and comfort. (See Revelation 1:11; Jeremiah 36:18.)

Through song or with musical instrument -- (II Kings 3:15; I Chronicles 25:3; Colossians 3:16; Ephesians 5:19).

Why is prophecy to be judged?

I Corinthians 13:9 -- *"For we know in part, and we prophesy in part."*

I Thessalonians 5:20-21 -- *"Despise not prophesyings. Prove all things; hold fast that which is good."*

I Corinthians 14:29 -- *"Let the prophets speak two or three, and let the other judge."*

I John 4:1 -- *"Beloved, believe not every spirit, but try the spirits whether they are of God: because many false prophets are gone out into the world."*

These references show us that prophecy is still an imperfect gift. We must understand that all of God's dealings through man involve both the natural and supernatural elements. The purity of the prophecy therefore depends on the degree of yieldedness to God. As long as we are human, there will always be the possibility of mixture. This is why we have need for controls, and the weighing or judging of prophecy.

There are three spirits potentially involved in prophecy:

the human spirit (Jeremiah 23:16; Ezekiel 13:3);

the Holy Spirit (I Corinthians 12:3, 7-10; I Timothy 4:1);

evil spirits (I Timothy 4:1-2; II Timothy 2:25-26; Ephesians 2:1-3).

Who is to judge prophecy?

* **Every believer who has the Spirit within him** -- The actual ability to discern error will vary according to levels of maturity and experience (I John 2:27; I Corinthians 2:15; I Thessalonians 5:21; John 10:27). The Lord has given His sheep an uncanny ability to recognize His voice. That inner witness of His Spirit is a comfort to us all.

* **The elders of the local assembly** -- (Hebrews 13:17; II Timothy 4:1-3; I Timothy 5:17; Ephesians 4:11-16).

* **Those with the gift of discernment** -- (I Corinthians 12:3, 10).

* **Prophets** -- (I Corinthians 14:29).

    Note: The New Testament prophets ministered in plurality for the purpose of confirming each other's messages (Acts 11:27; 13:1; I Corinthians 14:29).

How is prophecy to be judged?

* **By the Word of God** -- (Hebrews 4:12; Revelation 22:18; I Corinthians 14:37; Isaiah 8:19-20; I Timothy 6:3; II Timothy 1:13; 3:16-17; II John 7-11).

* **By the witness of the Spirit** -- Not only will it agree with the letter, but also with the spirit of the Word. This will be witnessed by the inner witness of the Holy Spirit in both the shepherd and the flock (I John 2:27; I Corinthians 2:15).

* **By the confession of Jesus Christ** -- (I John 4:1-3; I Corinthians 12:3).

* **By its fruit** -- Does it edify and produce life and liberty? Is it a clear sound, or a confused sound? Does the one prophesying manifest the fruit of the Spirit (Galatians 5:22-26)?

* **By the fulfillment of the prophecy** --

Deuteronomy 18:21-22 -- *"And if thou say in thine heart, How shall we know the word which the Lord hath not spoken? When a prophet speaketh in the name of the Lord, if the thing follow not, nor come to pass, that is the thing which the Lord hath not spoken, but the prophet hath spoken it presumptuously: thou shall not be afraid of him."*

Note: God allows the false to continue, and even to come within the walls of His church for the purpose of adding clarity and vividness to the truth. Thus we learn well by the contrast. He also uses the occasion of error to vindicate His true servants and openly manifest who are His appointed leaders among His people (Deuteronomy 13:1-5; I Corinthians 11:19).

At times it is in order in a public assembly for the pastor or a senior elder to evaluate and interpret to the people what the previous prophecies have said. In this way, he can clarify and summarize the message of the Spirit for that meeting and add his own sense of direction and then lead the people in prayer as a corporate response to the Spirit's message. This weighing and interpreting of prophetic utterances is an important aspect of the public judging of prophecies. During this time, the pastor can point out to the people what was of God by emphasizing it. If something has been said that was questionable, he can partly correct the error by simple omission or by going around it. If the error was serious enough of a threat to the body, he can make public correction of it. If it was of a less serious nature, he can deal with it privately.

Other Pertinent Questions

Is everyone who prophesies a prophet?

It is clear as we study the New Testament that there is a distinct difference between the gift of prophecy for every believer and the office of a prophet. The manifestation of prophecy spoken of in I Corinthians 12 and 14 is clearly an expression of the Spirit that is to take place through the various members of the body. The prophet, however, as spoken of in Ephesians 4:7-11, is himself referred to as a gift to the body (as are all the gift ministries).

When the scripture makes reference to prophesy at times it refers to the gift of prophecy that is accessible to every believer (I Corinthians 12:10; 14:16, 24, 31; Acts 21:9) and at other times it refers to those who have been called to the office of a prophet (Acts 13:1; 14:32). Prophesying refers to a gift or manifestation of the Spirit; prophet refers to a man.

Is prophecy to be directive in itself, or confirmative?

We notice that there is very little evidence that the apostles depended on prophecies for major decisions and guidance. Even in Acts 13:1-5, the prophetic word only confirmed the calling of Paul that had been previously spoken (Acts 9:15). The direction of a prophetic word should confirm what the Lord has already been impressing on us.

What should I do if someone speaks a personal prophecy over me that confuses me or that I do not witness to?

Again, personal guidance was never a major function of prophecy. Paul was told over and over by prophecy that bond and afflictions awaited him at Jerusalem. Yet that prophetic knowledge was not his guidance (Acts 20:22-24; 21:10-14). Generally, guidance comes to a person directly, only being confirmed by others.

In such a case as mentioned in the question, it should just be *put on the shelf* and confirmation awaited. The Lord never objects to our earnest desire for confirmation. He, in fact, tells us that everything should be confirmed in the mouth of two or three witnesses (II Corinthians 13:1).

What Bible references are used to teach that prophecy has ceased?

Probably the main passage that is used to teach this is I Corinthians 13:8-13. It is said that this passage teaches that *"that which is perfect"* came with the completion of the canon of Scripture, and the gifts of the Spirit (prophecy, tongues) have become antiquated.

However, Paul is speaking a truth that is mentioned by him often: the fact that the church is growing into full manhood and maturity; that the body is growing up into the head and will find its perfect completion (Ephesians 4:13-16). Paul is contrasting that which is perfect (mature) with that which is in part, fragmentary; or immature. In verse 11 of I Corinthians 13, he contrasts childhood with manhood. This corresponds with his analogy in Ephesians 4:13-14.

The concept that we do not need prophecy because the Scriptures are completely written is not valid. The purpose of prophecy was never just to write Scripture. Probably much more prophecy was spoken and not recorded by the prophets than was recorded.

Also, even though the Word of God is completely written, it has not completely been fulfilled. And the way God brings this fulfillment is largely through speaking the Word into the life of the church afresh. God always speaks things into being. If we take away His voice, we take away the *"word of His power"* to get us where we are going (Hebrews 1:3).

What are examples of things in my life that will contaminate my prophesies?

One of the major areas is the *"root of bitterness,"* which defiles many (Hebrews 12:5; James 3:11-14; Colossians 3:19; Ephesians 4:31).

We could say anything which touches a major negative attitude in your life will pollute the flow of prophecy. It is not the water that is dirty, but the pipeline. The water is tainted by the vessel. Some other areas are pride, depression, antagonism, an unyielding and stubborn attitude, an independent spirit, rebelliousness, dogmatism. All these attitudes can be picked up in everything one does, even the operation of the gifts.

What are some of the major reasons believers hold back from prophesying?

* Fear --

Fear of people (faces).

Fear of missing God and saying something wrong or something just from their own minds.

Fear that their faith will fail (break down) in the middle of the prophecy.

Fear of their own voice.

II Timothy 1:7 -- *"God hath not given us the spirit of fear; but of power, and of love, and of a sound mind."*

170

* By mentally pushing prophesying out of reach. Taking the attitude that it is beyond their ability to ever achieve. This making spiritual things unattainable and over-complicated is often based on a low self-image or self-rejection.

* By not staying exposed to an environment where prophecy is flowing.

* By not living in the Word. If the Word of Christ is not dwelling in a person richly, then the Spirit has little to draw from.

* By wanting to start at the top; the desire to be deep and profound rather than stick to the simple. A perfectionist is often easily discouraged at this point. This can also be a motivating factor that causes one to try to prophesy beyond his faith and maturity or to be over-dramatic and authoritative when prophesying. He feels that the profundity or the authoritative way in which he speaks, or the volume and enthusiasm with which he speaks, will make the prophecy more important and have greater impact. It is the motivation of the person and the actual level of the anointing which are the issues.

What are some practical points of wisdom that are to govern prophesying in the assembly?

(Also refer back to Chapter 16 of this book.)

* Refrain from scolding, lecturing, or whipping people through prophecy. This also applies to extremely negative, harsh or judgmental prophesying.

* Avoid prophesying your pet doctrines and favorite emphases.

* Avoid the temptation to give out personal counselling to some need of which you happen to be aware.

* Avoid correcting the leadership through prophecy.

* Avoid introducing a brand new direction into the service through prophecy.

* Avoid preaching for extended periods while prophesying, by elaborating or expanding on the message after the anointing lifts.

* Refrain from redundant or repetitive prophecies. When the mind of God has been clearly communicated through several messages already, do not jump in and say it over, but let it remain clear, concise and powerful. The force of prophecy is dissolved through wordiness.

* Stay in the tune and tenor of the meeting. Do not go cross-current or against the current. This frustrates and obstructs the message the Lord wants spoken. If a conflict develops and two or more separate veins are flowing, then the leadership must be responsible for coming in and leading the meeting as they feel the Spirit is leading.

* Refrain from yelling, screaming, whining or other extremes in voice or manner. The ideal is to speak inspirationally, but observing all the common laws of communication (good grammar, pronunciation, tone, etc.). This is where *"all things be done decently and in order"* (I Corinthians 14:40).

The *"spirit of the prophet is subject to the prophet"* (I Corinthians 14:32) principle applies here. God leaves man in full control. Yielding to trances and ecstasies, or some state where control is lost, is what the spiritualists and other cults practice. A fruit of the Spirit is self-control. He does not take that away, but rather gives it.

* Refrain from injecting self and personal problems into your prophecy: moods, pressures or circumstances, empty heartedness, anger, irritation, hastiness, opinions.

It is important to have any negative elements purged from

your own spirit. Avoid speaking on issues where you know you still have negative emotional involvement.

* Refrain from speaking if you have an unclear or obscure message. If the trumpet makes uncertain sound, it produces confusion (I Corinthians 14:33,40; 14:4-12).

* Stick to the Word. This is especially true for beginners. Do not swim out too far from shore until you are sure your vessel is itself well-established. The Spirit Himself seems to somewhat confine beginners to prophesying the written Word itself with very few other comments. He thus takes a word from the Word and makes it live for a given occasion.

Related to this is the principle of staying within your measure of faith. The greatest possible good is received from your prophecies when you stay within the limits of your own faith and maturity (Romans 12:6).

24

What is the "Gift of Diverse Kinds of Tongues and Interpretation of Tongues"?

We will first limit ourselves to the actual gifts of tongues and interpretation of tongues in the public assembly, then go on to consider the subject of speaking in tongues in a general way.

What is the gift of diverse kinds of tongues?

The gift of tongues is the God-given enablement to communicate in a language one does not know, to be interpreted in the assembly that all may understand.

I Corinthians 12:10 -- *"...to another divers kinds of tongues; to another the interpretation of tongues."*

Again, this is a *"manifestation of the Spirit"* (I Corinthians 12:7), and not human ability. It has absolutely nothing to do with natural linguistic ability, eloquence of speech, or a new sanctified way of talking. Though the Spirit may be involved in and produce all these, they are all separate from the subject at hand. The gift of tongues is a supernatural manifestation or expression of the Holy Spirit through a person's speech organs. It is a direct manifestation of the miraculous.

Does this differ from tongues as they are used in the believer's private life?

The Bible clearly reveals three general categories of speaking in tongues.

* Tongues spoken at the time the Spirit is received (Acts 2:4-6; 10:45-47; 19:6).

* Tongues for personal communion with God on a continual basis (I Corinthians 14:1-4, 15; Jude 20; Romans 8:26-27; Ephesians 6:18).

* Tongues given in the assembly to communicate to the body and be a sign to the unbeliever (I Corinthians 12:10; 14:5, 21-22).

Also, we should understand that there are three general ways the Bible uses the word *"gift"* or *"grace"*:

* God's *"gift"* of salvation through Christ (Romans 5:15-18; II Corinthians 9:15), which includes:

* The *"gift"* of the Holy Spirit (Acts 2:38; 8:20; 10:45), which includes:

* The *"gifts"* of the Holy Spirit (I Corinthians 12:1, 4, 9, 28; 14:1; Hebrews 2:4).

Paul teaches that speaking in tongues is for private and person use in prayer and praise and self-edification. But there are those whom the Spirit prompts to speak in the gift of tongues in the assembly, to be then interpreted, to bless the people.

The gift of tongues is for edifying the church, not the individual who exercises it. Speaking in tongues as a part of the gift of the Holy Spirit is to continue in the personal life for individual edification, not that of the church.

What are the purposes of tongues and interpretation in the assembly?

* To be a *"sign"* to the unbeliever (I Corinthians 14:21-22).

* To speak edification, exhortation and comfort to the believer (I Corinthians 14:3-5). Tongues with interpretation are equal to prophecy.

* To lift the congregation into praise or prayer (I Corinthians 14:13-16). Here Paul encourages one who speaks in tongues to pray for interpretation. The immediate context that follows is praying and praising in tongues. The implication is that prayer and praise in the Spirit could be interpreted and be edifying to the body.

In what ways are tongues a "sign" to unbelievers?

* **By the evidence of the supernatural** -- seeing people speak languages they have never learned (Acts 2:6-8; I Corinthians 14:21-22).

* **By the sense of the supernatural** -- it charges the atmosphere with the sense of God's presence. This is felt even by unbelievers (Acts 2:1; Acts 3:19; Acts 2:47).

* **By the witness of hearing a foreign language they may know** -- God gives them a sign by speaking to them in their native tongue (or another tongue they have learned). He may speak that which applies personally, unveiling the heart of the unbeliever. This was the great sign at Pentecost. They heard people speak supernaturally in their own native tongues. The sign led to the salvation of three thousand souls (Acts 2).

Is everyone to have the gift of diverse kinds of tongues?

I Corinthians 12:28-30 clearly shows that all are not used in this way. Though all might step out on occasions by faith and speak in diverse tongues, it is not Scriptural to teach that everyone is to have the same gift of the Spirit. This was one of Paul's main emphases in his teaching on the gifts and body ministry (Romans 12:3-8; I Corinthians 12:4-31).

How many messages in tongues and interpretations are in order in one meeting?

The answer to this is given very simply and briefly by Paul in I Corinthians 14:27-28. Two or three messages are usually sufficient to receive with clarity the full drift of what the Lord is saying. Scripture does not tell us to silence the messages in assembly life, but rather to regulate them. We have, in fact, the direct admonition: *"Forbid not to speak in tongues"* (I Corinthians 14:39-40).

What is the gift of interpretation of tongues?

The gift of interpretation is the supernatural, spontaneous ability to interpret a communication given in tongues into the language understood by the people present. Again, it has absolutely nothing to do with natural knowledge of languages, but comes directly from the Holy Spirit (I Corinthians 12:10). Notice I Corinthians 14:13 says *"pray that he may interpret,"* not study language. Also I Corinthians 14:12 shows that when one speaks in tongues, *"no man understandeth him."* It, therefore, must be supernaturally revealed, just as the message in tongues was supernatural. The interpretation should be given in immediate response to the message in tongues.

Is interpretation the same as translation?

To interpret means to explain, expound, or to unfold. To translate means to convert from one language into another. Actually, the degree of actual translation may vary according to the particular gift of interpretation. Also we should remember that even to translate from one language to another often leaves a great discrepancy between the length of the message and number of words required to say the same thing. Notice in Daniel 5:25-28 that the interpretation of *"Mene, mene, tekel, upharsin,"* was about nine times as long as the original message.

Another reason that messages may be much shorter than their interpretations is that the situation actually involves tongues followed by a prophecy; or it may be a prayer in tongues followed by a response from the Lord by way of prophecy.

We should also mention that a message in tongues may actually be prayer or worship, as well as exhortation. Often a person will speak out a Spirit-inspired prayer which God wants lifted at that time. The interpretation then informs the people regarding that which was prayed and lifts them into prayer together as well as stirring their faith. At other times, the Lord may desire His people to praise and worship Him and prompt one to lead out in tongues. When interpreted, it lifts the people into praise and worship. If real interpretation is taking place, therefore, some of the messages in tongues will undoubtedly be interpreted as prayers and praise, as well as exhortation.

The possible explanations for the fact that some messages in tongues are followed by prophecy instead of interpretation might be: possibly the message in tongues was out of order and inspired someone else to prophecy; someone jumped in and prophesied before an interpretation could be given; because there was no interpreter present, or the one with the interpretation would not give it so someone with a gift of prophecy moved in. With regard to this last possible reason, it is not clear to some that there is any difference between the gift of prophecy and the gift of interpretation. They, therefore, may attempt to interpret messages in tongues just because they prophesy. There is, however, a definite difference and it must be respected.

What messages does one interpret?

Whether interpretation is needed or not depends on the setting and category of tongues being spoken. There were no interpretations ever given when people spoke in tongues upon receiving the Holy Spirit (Acts 2:4-6; 10:45-47; 19:6). Also, Scripture indicates that when tongues are used for personal prayer or worship, they are not interpreted (I Corinthians 14:2, 14-18, Romans 8:26-27).

The only tongues Paul said needed interpretation are ones spoken in the church with the purpose of communicating to men. Usually this will be self-evident. One person, during a lull in the worship or quiet time of prayer and waiting on God, will distinctly lift his voice for a short time, speaking in a tongue unknown to those present. This is in the category of *"divers kinds of tongues"* which needs to be interpreted (I Corinthians 12:10; 14:12-13).

Who is to interpret tongues in the assembly?

Basically, one to whom the gift has been given should do the interpreting. It may be one other than the one giving the message in tongues (I Corinthians 14:27). Or it may be the one who spoke the message in tongues (I Corinthians 14:5, 13).

It is clear in Scripture that the one exercising the gift of tongues should also seek the interpretation of that tongue (I Corinthians 14:1-5,13). Paul seemed to indicate in I Corinthians 14:27 that in any given meeting it is in order for one person to do the interpreting.

Probably more emphasis needs to be put on the gift of interpretation of tongues. It seems to have been a neglected area of understanding in the past. Actually not just everyone and anyone should attempt it. The attempts to interpret by those who did not specifically have that gift are probably why there have not been more pure interpretations.

Also, it is significant for those who give messages in tongues to realize that their responsibility does not end with just speaking out in tongues if no one is present with the gift of interpretation. The responsibility then falls back on them to interpret their own words, or to be out of order (I Corinthians 14:5, 13, 28).

How do I know if I am to give a message in tongues or interpretation?

Sensitivity to the Spirit's inner promptings is an area we must all learn. It is more in the subjective realm than the objective; no list of rules can be produced to tell us how it is done.

We must realize that Jesus did not judge or reject His disciples for making mistakes when they were trying to do His will. The terror of the consequences of one minor mistake may cause a person to avoid involvement permanently. God has patience with us when our hearts are pure and we are earnestly seeking to do His will. Just as parents watching their child learn to walk, so the Lord watches over us as we stumble or falter along learning to walk in spiritual gifts.